Put Me in the River
Sevda Khatamian

Copyright © 2020 Sevda Khatamian
All rights reserved.
ISBN: 9798681900719

To my limited budget...

In One Minute

    I didn't know about the time, only the sun was up. The bright sunlight woke me up, not that I could really do it on my own. The light was so sharp that forced open my eyes. I was still in the middle of my sleep, perhaps partially paralyzed since I couldn't hold my head straight on the neck. I struggled, but the effort was in vain. I let go, decided to try again in one minute. Closed my eyes to the sunlight, & watched the colors change behind my eyelids; pale orange turn into white, yellow, red, orange, and then white again. I was sitting by the window on a relatively small airplane. It was the first journey of a rather long trip which I'm going to tell you more about in one minute. I do recall being strangely excited and thrilled, meanwhile, uncertain and anxious for a brand new future I was landing on. I assumed I had a clue what was going to happen; I didn't. Regardless, I was too exhausted to distinguish one from two, let alone solving riddles of the upcoming times. All I wanted was to get some more sleep, yet, I was supposed to wake up.

I opened my eyes for a few seconds here and there, tried glancing out the window to come back to reality. The view would vary whenever I had a look; for one second, it was an endless ocean of clouds in all kinds of shapes and colors, in one minute it would be nothing but the blue sea. I couldn't possibly tell where we were. I could see small towns surrounded in forests and lakes. They were the suburbs of a bigger city. According to my calculations on the clock, that we were about to land soon, we should've been passing the territories of the neighboring country. Soon we would pass the sea, & would reach the airport amongst the colorful trees of mid-autumn.

The airplane window was too small for the horizon, yet its glory wasn't diminished. I watched the sun rising gradually above the skyline as I fell in & out of sleep. The sun was deep yellow which was getting whiter and brighter by the second. It was fully up in the sky when I finally awoke. It felt like it all happened in one minute. But, the sunrise takes much longer in reality. The sky was now light blue, & there were few clouds beneath. Depending on the angle of the sunlight, they'd take on different colors. I let myself be amazed by them.

I still had to squint hard to see outside, not only because of the severe light, but for I'd just got up, & my body wasn't yet ready. I yawned, rubbed my face with the palms of my hands, stretched to every possible side on my small airplane seat; I needed time. It was pure luck that nobody was sitting by me, which barely happens. Well, happened, in the past, the world is kind of upside-down these days. Airlines and airways have scheduled a new working system after the epidemic of infectious disease. Having the board half-empty used to be considered as a rare occasion. Of course, it depended on the route, the time of the year, the airline, or how popular the destination was. But, traveling by aeroplanes, in general, had become widely accessible that a small incident such as an empty seat next to you was so extraordinary to bring great joy to the trip, especially, if you're always as tired as I am, & you'd need to lay your body horizontally to get proper rest. Airplane tickets didn't cost as much as they used to, let's say ten years before. The airports were much busier, then, so were the planes. Sometimes they would even be overbooked which only meant they needed to leave someone behind.

There's a naïve pleasure in meeting strangers brought randomly to the trip. I look forward to being surprised by getting a glimpse of how it could be lived differently, by learning new ways of seeing. Sharing the ride with a stranger could indeed be a curious thing: in cars, planes, trains, or buses. Usually, as I get to the check-in counter at the airport, to drop off my luggage and get my boarding pass, I scan the queue to guess my next-door neighbor; I'm almost never right, though it's more of a fun game to pass the time, imagine with whom I'll be traveling with. I'm usually one of the last people to get on board, so my fellow passenger would already be sitting comfortably on their seat when I arrive. I would say hello to them as I take my seat, would greet them with a smile. Then, I'd either appreciate their help on putting my black rucksack on the overhead compartment, or would apologize for the discomfort I'd caused by shoving the bag underneath the front seat. The hardest part is to break the invisible bubble surrounding the people I newly meet. I used to shy away from making conversations, however, meeting many different people along the way, especially older citizens of the countryside who are unembarrassed enough to talk to anyone anywhere had inspired me to draw the bubble off without much hesitation. The key to breaking the barrier lies underneath asking questions. However, the starting point to follow the recipe depends on if we spoke a language in common. I take another approach if verbal communication is not the case; otherwise, I keep asking questions about different things in order to know enough about the new friend. The goal is to ultimately feel comfortable in my new environment. Sometimes a couple questions would do. Sometimes, one question leads to another, & we end up in a long sincere conversation.

I would ask them if they're going, or if they're on their way back. Even though the answer is quite obvious, I'd ask them if they travel alone; it usually makes enough time to come up with the next question. Being the questioner means that I wouldn't have to answer as much. Not that I'm holding a big secret or some of that kind; certain questions would be too confusing to answer briefly. Even a question as simple as what I was doing in life could get my voice shaking out of horror; it was a mystery to me as well. My world seemed to be turning on its head. I had been freshly scrubbed, physically, and psychologically. Even the air felt different for what I knew.

It's a long story. Not so sure if I could call it a story; the story wouldn't begin until it ended. There was a moment that a great discomfort arrived all of a sudden, disappointment, a heart that was broken. And a landlord who asked to have the apartment back. I took the move as my good luck charm. Moved and readjusted to my new living space, only to find out that the discomfort wouldn't go anywhere; I was still not happy with my time. The change wasn't major enough, it appeared to me that I had to lean toward a more radical change. Things had to be stirred up until the right consistency was achieved.

I started to eliminate my stuff to somehow get lighter. There were only two options, really. Either sell, or donate to people whom I thought might need them. The secret third option was to place them neatly on the side of the trash bin down the street, hoping someone in need would come across them. Living in such a big City, somebody was always in need of something. My most valuable belongings were delicately packed, sent to the trusted places to keep safe, mainly to put them on pause for a while, hopefully, to deal with later in a more peaceful state of mind. The blue suitcase was filled with clothes and shoes and things that I used to live with, mugs and towels and my electric kettle. In the end, it had to travel to my parents alongside a few shoulder bags, & a couple of boxes.

The small brown suitcase which was responsible for holding more practical things was staying in the City with Sahan, a friend of mine, until I was back from the first journey. If the plan was to move about, I realized, then, I had to purchase another suitcase. The ideal plan was to pack, leave, and return years later, when everything had a new face, & life had changed so drastically that it wouldn't remember you anymore. But, that wasn't really possible. In reality, the visa expires sooner or later, & you have to come back, whether or not you would want to move elsewhere. It's a must; a visa is an approval to let you discover other lands.

Didam, a friend of mine, and I headed to the marketplace looking for decent luggage. We had to find the suitcase's corner first. Even though exploring a market is one of the greatest funs, discovering the whole area was out of our time and patience; the trip was cut short. We found a few stores near each other, full of camping backpacks and suitcases; we decided that we wouldn't find a deal any better. Outside by the front door, I noticed a suitcase with a hard plastic shell; the water wouldn't leak through. It was sitting quietly and diagonally; it would hold its structural integrity for all the times where the circumstances would be a bit too rough on it. The wheels would rotate three-sixty-five; quite nice and easy to take it around with.

More than the suitcase itself, it was the owner of the store who intrigued us to step closer to have a look. He was an old man, one of those old men with a kind face and a warm voice. He was chatting with a friend as he was fixing a bag on his lap; they were drinking tea. He must've had a good sense of humor because I remember them laughing at whatever he was saying. He exhibited a few models, eventually showcased the one that my eyes had zoomed and focused. I was quite hesitant about the color of the suitcase. There were two options: black and yellow. It took me few good minutes to finally decide. They looked equally attractive in a way that made me want to have them both. It was a hard decision, I only needed one.

The black one, it was. I imagined taking it with me everywhere, even though I had no idea where. It was a tragic misfortune that I lost the black suitcase at a very early stage of the trip. We could call that an innocent accident, let's call it that. It was not lost completely, but physically speaking, damaged enough that I had to let it rest.

One of the wheels broke on my way back from this trip, the first journey. I was waiting around the luggage delivery ring at the airport, looking forward to the black suitcase to show from behind the plastic curtains. My phone rang in my pocket; Didam was on the other end of the line. I was telling her that the plane had landed, we'd be meeting soon. The black suitcase drew the curtain effortlessly, & glided to me. Very excited to see it again, I prepared myself to pick it up. I guess I was distracted with the conversation, or I might've forgotten how heavy it was. Oh, it was heavy! I held the handle, pulled it toward myself. It was hard to maneuver the load with one hand, so I dropped it. Consequently, one of the wheels broke. I didn't realize it was damaged at first, although, I did hear something breaking as the luggage landed. The suitcase wasn't walking with me, which got me seriously worried. I examined the broken wheel; it wasn't manufactured to be repaired again. The whole thing was off. Isn't that the way everything is these days?! It's impossible to get things fixed; once they break, they're out, & they need to be put aside for good.

Luckily, the suitcase didn't completely go dysfunctional. Actually, it was perfect for storing my leftovers back in the City; I should've thought of it from the beginning. As I was away during the first journey, everything was tightly squeezed in the small brown suitcase. The stuff that were used less frequently, but were too precious to put on the side of the trash bin: jackets and boots and a pocket knife. There was a lesson to embrace in the broken wheel of the black suitcase, honoring the innocence of the misfortune: travel light, but I don't think I ever take my lesson.

Being heavy was not the case for the black suitcase only, they were all so: the blue backpack, the gray or the Tanzender rucksack, the brown suitcase, even the funky red which was rather a daypack. In fact, if there were any lessons to be learned regarding the weight of the load, it was during the forest fire when the house had to be evacuated and all the rest of the story which I'm going to talk about soon. I certainly didn't need that amount, materials and souvenirs and more than enough clothes. I couldn't resist. There must've been a comfort, a sense of security in dragging heavy luggage behind me, or to have them on my person. Certain things had to travel with me, otherwise, the trip wouldn't be the same. Who's to tell?! Regardless, I sure could've toned it down a bit, stay lighter, even if it was only one less shirt, for the sake of my right knee, the wheel of the black suitcase, or the belt of the blue bag.

My fellow passengers wondered the very typical thought, what I was doing, which was usually responded very vaguely. I would only tell them that I was doing alright.

If, naturally, if a conversation ever occurred; sometimes we wouldn't even speak the same language. We'd simply sit next to each other quietly; a plain smile would do, or pointing at something beautiful I'd noticed out the window. As a matter of fact, remaining silent was a major part of my trips. I was convinced that traveling alone would disclose independence and strength. And that it was so cool to discover all the new places on your own, quite liberating not to be reliant on others to make decisions throughout the trip; you do as you wish, you take whichever path you fancy.

However, it turned out it's not always as fun. Someone suggested that you'd make many new friends when you travel alone. You do, not that you don't. Wherever you go, you get to meet people, locals, or other travelers. And when the connection is right, it extends into other events in near future: a drink, dinner, or a picnic by the river. But eventually, you must part, you must say goodbye. That's where the friendship, the way you knew it before ends; it fades as soon as friends are out of sight. Some farewells are clear signs of an absolute end, and that you'll never hear from them again. Unless the universe pulls a trick, & connect you again somehow. But, sometimes you'd hug them goodbye, as you decide to stay in touch, occasionally send each other messages wishing good times. Then, you come across random shots of their lives online, their comments on a political statement, videos they've found to be funny. It is odd; somehow you were supposed to keep a simple correspondence, notice their gradual disappearance in time, & merely recall them as a sweet memory from one of the travels, instead of observing the stream of their lives. Then again, I can't really complain about it much. It's nice to know they are there, to see certain occasions of their lives, wondering if you'd meet up somewhere. And once in a blue moon, you hit a gem. One of these new friends would hold a dear place in the heart. The circumstances and the power of mankind bring you back together; it evolves into a long-lasting friendship.

Back at my small airplane seat, I couldn't possibly know traveling alone is not what they say it is. It has a mind of its own; not nearly as fun as taking a trip with friends and family, people that you share a common history with; the journey only adds up to the account. You know where to go, how to travel; you have more things to say, than just to introduce yourself over and over. It's a bit different when it comes to friends; they're not clothes or collection of random things. They exist consciously. Interestingly, online; easily accessible through a smartphone device. They're in the pocket, in a way, you could reach them as long as you're both connected to a network. You get to send them pictures, chat over a video call, send voice messages to have a moment together. It's a pleasure to speak with a friend, tell them things, & hear back from them.

Humans, however, weren't the only friends I made along the way; cats and dogs were a major part of this circle. Dogs seemed to be more challenging to decode. I was usually their casual hangout unless I spent a decent amount of time with them to raise myself to the close friends' level. Now that I think about the dogs I met, Karamel could be considered a good friend, Gorgin, or Shanti who took so long to finally consider me family. And, of course, Gaman who indeed was one. They were the guys that I took walks with, had them smell the area, & socialize with others. Time is the glue to bond the two parties together, to call it friendship; unfortunately, I never really had enough of it. Time.

The good news is that if a dog befriends you, you'll be remembered for good. Cats, on the other hand, seem to have no memories of you once you're gone for a while, or at least that's how they make it appear. They say cats don't have much of a memory, but I can't be so sure. Afro never deprived me of his kind greetings, standing quietly by my feet for a couple seconds as we meet, even though we only meet about once a year. Some cats would care and look after their human friends so much as if they're dogs of some kind.

Mr. Purhonen, for instance, was one of the friendliest cats I've ever met. Kind, caring, and loyal. He was a part of Merja and Raimo's big loving family, whom I met just a few hours after the airplane trip I was on. I got to live with them during the first journey. Mr. Purhonen was very warm and welcoming even from day one; an unlucky misfortune tightened the string between the two of us overnight.

It was past midnight when I paused the music on my computer, left the studio to go upstairs to my room for a late-night snack, anything that I could get my hands on in the cupboards of the kitchenette of my room, some biscuit, nuts, or something to munch on as I was working late. We'd already been alerted by the curious noises heard from the walls in the last few days, highly suspicious of mice breaking and entering.

We were fully aware of their existence in our enormous ancient household. What we didn't know was that they'd already found their way inside the cupboards to attack our food.

I opened the door of my room. Didn't bother turning the light on, I was staying in the room for about ten seconds if not less. I pulled the tall bottom drawer, grabbed the pack of the whole wheat biscuits, & turned around to go downstairs to the big kitchen to make some black tea. My fingertips felt the biscuit in the darkness, which was rather strange; I walked down the spiral staircase. I couldn't recall opening it before. I investigated the package from all sides and angles in the hallway as I passed the wide dinner table, and stood by the counter. The package hadn't been opened according to the instructions; it was torn apart from one corner, & few of the biscuits were chewed on; only an animal would've ripped it so. An animal?! There it hit me. I flipped over, freaked out, threw the innocent pack of biscuit onto the air which was only a victim of a naïve burglary. I started to shake my hand vigorously as if there was something nasty on the fingertips that had touched the chewed-up biscuit. I quite like mice, don't get me wrong; I find them to be very cute. They only become unpleasant when they're inside the house.

I looked around for help, I found none; everybody was in bed. Except for, you guessed it, Mr. Purhonen. He was standing in the corner of the kitchen, asking me what the matter was with his round eyes. I sat down on my knees next to him, and gave him a hug. I could've taken him to my bedroom with me to protect me from the immense horror that was floating in the air. But I decided to sleep on the couch in the studio; I was too terrified to go back to my room. Mr. Purhonen, of course, joined me on the sofa. His two other friends weren't around, Mr. Korhonen and Mrs. Raizanen, but I don't think they would've been as supportive. Mr. Purhonen was definitely the friendliest out of those three. Mr. Korhonen was only shy, took him a couple months to get used to me, or dare to come near me. And Mrs. Raizanen never really let her guards down. It might not be fair to generalize cats this easily, but it might be something about female cats. I noticed the same pattern in Amanda's behavior, or Maggie's.

Ararat and Volga were two other kind cats I met during the trips. A bit too kind, maybe. They were twin brothers who were living in the yard of the School. I believe they were traumatized by their mother when they were kittens; she truly hated them. The mother was actually Denisas's cat that would normally stay at Luís's who was away during the occasion. And considering the interactions between the mother and her children, they had to find a home for the kittens, which, in the end, happened to be the School.

I was first introduced to the family during the forest fire, when we had to escape the School, & shelter somewhere safe, which in this case would be Liudvika and Naja's house in Kinta down the village. Although, I'm not so sure how safe the house really was since the gas station was only a few hundred steps away. The cats were in the living room when we arrived, all three of them; it was late at night. And before we went to sleep, Naja explained about the sleeping arrangements, & that we had to keep the mother separate from the twins throughout the night, otherwise it was going to be a disaster. I picked the couch as my bed, RJ slept on the floor by the balcony door. I believe the baby cats stayed with Naja during the night, & the mother was kept in the other room upstairs. The mother couldn't stand her children, she couldn't stop hissing at the poor creatures for some cruel reason. Her great hate and aggression toward them had affected them majorly, which arose to the surface as the kittens grew into adult cats. I noticed their bizarre behavior a few months later in my return to the School, the kind of behavior that you wouldn't expect from any cats.

Ararat & Volga were busy growing up during the few months that I was exploring the southern regions. And, of course, I met two other cats meanwhile, which, to be honest, I can't really recall their names. I'm not so good with names, maybe I've mentioned that before, I don't remember. The gray one must've been Pesecu, but I'm not so sure about the ginger cat. He was chubbier, rather less curious, & a bit lazier. I would've known them better if I'd spent more time with them. There were only a few mutual experiences. When Sara and Carlos were away, the owners of the house, I would look for them in the yard before I closed the kitchen door for the night, just to make sure they were back home safe and sound. I would leave them food and snacks, make sure they had enough water.

One stormy winter's night, I came back from the studio quite late, exhausted for the work, dripping from the horrid rain. The two cats ran downstairs as soon as they heard the key turning in the door. They looked frantic with fear, were indeed glad to see me back. Even Pesecu who was quite courageous & protective was terrified about something. I assumed it was the rain, the loud wind, the growling of the thunders to frighten them so, & that the storm had attacked such dry land so suddenly. As soon as I reached upstairs, I was illuminated with the truth. The tall window in the corner of the living room had flapped open. Wide open, from floor to ceiling, it felt as we were having the storm in the living room; the rain was pouring inside. The long curtain was flying all over the room, & the rugs were soaking wet. I forced the old rusted window shut, closed the solid shutters on the inside, bolted both windows tightly. I gave the two cats a warm hug to let them know everything was fine; it indeed was a scary incident.

Ararat and Volga weren't kittens anymore once I was back in the School. In fact, it took me quite a bit to realize that the cats were the same ones I'd met back in Kinta. They were officially residing in the School. I have to admit, now that I think about it, I could've been kinder with them when I was living with them. I was told that I wouldn't have to let them in. So, that's what I did, I kept them out. We were concerned that they would jump on the tables with their muddy paws, would walk on the kitchen counter, & would eat our food off the cutting board or the plate. I mean, these are not such pleasant behaviors, but, so what if they did?! All they ever wanted was the company of a human, a warm shelter to get them through the tough winter, and food to comfort their unfortunate soul. I could've given the tables a wipe if they took a walk on them, and ask them kindly to stop doing that.

Although, I was nice enough with them all the while, therefore, soon we became close friends. So close that I dropped a few tears when we found out that Ararat was gone. They're cats. Obviously, they roam about, especially around springtime when the hormones start to run wild. Sometimes they would disappear for a day or two, although, I don't believe Volga ever really left the School. But Ararat would wander periodically, & would show up all exhausted and drenched for the adventurous trip. His absence would get us worried, but in the end, he would return one way or another. Except for that one time, when he took off, & wasn't seen ever after. At least, not for a very long while. We waited, hoping that he'd come back soon, but there were no signs of him.

We each developed our theories of the on-going problem. A car accident was the worst-case scenario, a loving marriage was the best. It was hard to imagine his dead body on the side of the road, so we kept on with our investigations. Every black and white cat around the village was a potential suspect. Ararat had a cute face with soft round lines; the village cats had more angular features. Luís was doing his own researches, experimenting with different methods to find him back, such as leaving food near the School, or calling his name around the valley, believing simply he would hear; we all hoped the same.

I spotted a cat that looked very similar to Ararat. The black and white spots on the back, the tail, & the shape of the body were the first clues to let me assume that we had a solid case. I kept following the new cat around the village to make sure that it was him. I would call his name out loud to get him to look back. Seeing his face would've been enough evidence to approve his identity, but he just wouldn't turn back. I kept encouraging him to return to us through different tricks. And, he finally showed up. It was later in the afternoon that I saw him in the corner of the left-hand terrace, devouring the cat food in the small white bowl. His paws and face were wounded. He seemed to be exhausted, as if he was fresh off a hard battle. Rather skinny too, I must say, I don't believe he had enough to eat. He was a home cat, of course, it would've been challenging for him to look after himself in the wild. He was fairly aggressive, furious about something that we couldn't know what; he was now mean.

Even his voice was totally different. Nothing was really the same about him anymore. Luís kept joking about it when I started to doubt if he was actually Ararat. He would say that they all change when they become a man. That was a funny joke, & we had a few good laughs, but the wrong cat was still in our School.

In the end, we realized that it wasn't even a 'he', it was a 'she' all the while; we were too desperate to notice. I went back to one of the pictures I took of the twins and myself. To my surprise, I found none of the spots on his face to be the same. It wasn't our cat, it didn't even look like him a hair; she was just a stranger, now, almost impossible to get rid of. Well, she was a nice cat. As a matter of fact, quite adorable and lovely. But she wasn't ours. A few weeks after, the wanted case was spotted by the supermarket. According to Luís, Ararat was witnessed walking carefree by the parking lot of the main grocery shop in the town. A big round of applause for his courage; he had journeyed about four kilometers away. He had claimed his independency, hopefully, was living a prosperous life.

Volga stayed with us, & we maintained our friendship effectively. We would take naps on the sofa, or on the bench down in the yard. He'd follow me around, call out to me when he was hungry. I was trying to be a good friend, to treat him nicely as much as I could. At some point, I seriously considered taking him with me wherever I went; too bad my bag was already overfull.

I have to say that I miss Volga often, I think about him occasionally. I receive pictures from friends, Bea or Filipe, who visited the School now and again for as long as the School existed, which only reminds me what a naïve cat he was. Kirke, however, holds the flag amongst all. The incident that we had to go through together was too intense to forget, at least on my end. It was her second stay at my Cottage whilst Domas was away. She was a shy one, her timing was different. It would take a couple days for her to get used to you, get comfortable, & come take an elegant nap on your lap. By then, I was rather familiar with her patterns. She was a playful cat. A princess, rather. She would spend most of her day outside, even though it was the dead of winter. One evening around dinnertime, as another mad storm was coming to an end, she came home quietly. She seemed to be really tired, so she jumped on the bed, & fell asleep right away. She closed her eyes, & wandered off in her dream world. She didn't even move on my lap when I joined her later at night. She didn't eat anything, didn't drink water. She seemed to have lost appetite, perhaps because of the extreme exhaustion; it may happen. There was not much to worry about. She's a cat, she knows better how to take care of herself. I thought maybe she was feeling homesick, maybe she was missing Domas and Enrika, or Eglė for all I knew; she wanted to be home soon. I put her on my lap, gently brushed her back, told her that it was going to be alright if she ever understood what that even meant.

She woke up the next day feeling the same, even worse, sick and tired of what was troubling her. Later in the afternoon, as I was having a cup of tea, I heard a change in her breathing. Sad deep breaths, crying quietly for help. She was obviously in great pain. Too bad we couldn't speak about it. For a few moments,

I was absolutely incapable of helping her. I held her, brought her the bowls of water and the dried food. She was limping on her right leg, I noticed, wondered how come I hadn't realized it the night before. She must've been into a fight with a fox or some other cat in the field. I gave the foot a quick look. Nothing seemed to be wrong, no evidence of wound or external injuries. I had to ask for help; things were getting serious.

The real problem, however, was that my network connection was out for over a week already, there was no way to communicate with Domas from my house. I didn't know anyone in the village, & the nearest neighbor to me was five minutes away on foot. It was the state of absolute solitude, which didn't make much sense in such a condition; we needed help. I kissed Kirke on the neck, told her that I'd be back in one minute. Grabbed my jacket, made sure the gloves were in the pockets, put on Merja's elf woolen beanie, and wrapped its funky tail around my neck. Bolting the door after me, I ran outside. I went to Arturas, hoping that they'd be home. Arturas and his family were almost the only people I knew in the village by then. I had met Albertas in front of my door, so technically, I didn't know where he lived. I knocked; nobody was home, I knocked again. I toured around in the yard, held my phone up in the air to receive signals to connect to their network. In honest words, I was stealing their connection, but it sure didn't matter a second by then. I sent a few messages to Domas to let him know about us, no good condition; he should send someone over to my Cottage.

Kirke was still on the bed when I returned, just as I'd left her, breathing tensely as her life flashed before her eyes. I don't think I'd ever forget the look on her face, begging for help as she slowly and gradually lost control over her body; it was a mess. Albertas knocked on the door within few minutes; Domas had asked him to rescue us. He made a couple phone calls. Even though I didn't understand the language, I could tell what they were about. Another man arrived in one minute. We put Kirke on a green towel I found in the closet, & took her to the man's house which happened to be my nearest neighbor.

Zita was waiting for us at home in the kitchen. I didn't quite figure out if the man was Zita's husband or not, I was only curious. Zita put Kirke on the table as they were preparing some shots, or splitting some pills for her. I didn't understand what the medications were, but they were quite effective. Kirke was very calm afterward, relieved and relaxed; she could sit, drink some water, & lick the sour cream off Zita's fingertip. She was still limping on her right foot, but that was not a big deal comparing to what we had just been through.

I asked Zita if she was a veterinarian, how she knew about all that. She said she loved animals; she had several chickens, few dogs, & twenty cats. She well knew what she was doing.

Tadas happened to be in the village the next morning; he was the younger brother of Domas. We took Kirke to her doctor in the town. The doctor asked few questions about what had happened the night before. They ran some tests on her. They found a blood clot on her paw which was causing the strange limping. She was diagnosed with heart disease. They said she was already born with it. Not much we could do about, except to make sure she would take her new medication every day. The doctor told us that she probably didn't have much time left, a year or two, which was quite depressing. The saddest part was that only we knew about it, the humans, Kirke had no idea.

I rubbed my eyes with my fingertips to force myself to wake up. I looked out the window. The sun was bright, something I quite needed. I'd better be up, the plane was about to land. I couldn't possibly tell how close we were to landing, but the clock was saying that it was going to happen soon. I took a good look at the few pieces of fluffy clouds, took a moment to appreciate them from above. The views would change in one minute; we were slowly diving in.

I was in great need of a hot beverage, preferably some water, which was a decent indicator of the start of a new day. But, it was rather intimidating to ask for anything. Sometimes the flight crew would refuse to bring you what you've asked for because they say the plane is about to land. Who knows, maybe they don't feel like doing it, or they don't like the color of your hair, & they make up an excuse; you can never be sure about the rules and the logic behind them. Some would charge you for a glass of water; it's only a glass of water. Besides, I was a bit nervous at that moment; a funny conversation with a flight attendant was the last thing to ask for.

It felt odd, excitement and nervousness blitz roughly together. I was slowly falling into a hole, clueless how deep it was going to be, or what was waiting by the end of the line if there ever was an end to it. I had stepped into an act, & I was watching my very first play. The circumstances made me come up with an impulse decision to switch paths, & take another direction. It was some kind of reaction to the colossal wave of actions, a solution to come up with at the moment without really considering the consequences as if there won't be any. It was as being in the middle of a storm in open waters. The fatal ninth wave would arise high suddenly from beyond a range of waves, as a tough mountain to soon swallow the boat, & cast it away to the unknown. In order to survive, I had to un-hold, let the water take me with, hopefully to a safe shore somewhere. Any further struggles would've made things worse, would drag me down deeper, get me to drink more of that salty water; there's no room for a clumsy sailor.

The first getaway that occurred to me was to take a trip. As I pondered the matter more, it seemed to be the only one. If a trip was the only escape, then, what good would it do if I kept being terrified of doing it?! Doing it alone. Which was quite something to be afraid of, to be alone. Not knowing the right direction or which paths to avoid made me uneasy, moving without a map felt itchy; however, it wasn't the place to hesitate another second; the wave was approaching near. I was aware that some roads might lead to a dead-end; it scared me even more. The missing ingredient to make it a comfort food was the experience of walking by a path going nowhere, & still enjoying its beauty. That it was quite alright to face nothing in the end. It was only time to warm my back up, to illuminate me with the broader image of the stage; they were all minutes and seconds of the show that had to be gratefully embraced.

Putting the trust in myself, & my limited budget, I went on with the road. The curiosity was raised afterward; it dawned on me so gradually. I was after something very vague that only got cleared as I stepped closer toward it. Walking gingerly in a dark room, let's say, not totally dark to get you blind, but quite dim to make the walk intimidating; you'd only see a couple steps ahead, would explore as you go further until you eventually get comfortable with the very little light in the room. You start learning about the room as you go on, where the table is, or how the chair is set by it. The more you know, the more encouraged you become to step on, perhaps to find out about the closet, or the bed, or if there's any kitchen in the room. The room expands with every step, you get to see beyond the darkness. Being alone in such a condition might spice things a bit; nobody to share the rush of adrenaline with. My mind must've been conquered by the tension, my body with a strong beat of the heart, which was only one of the first steps of traveling alone. It was odd to travel alone, I have to confess, intriguing and strange altogether. Within a few months, I found out that traveling alone is quite trendy, & people promote it all over the globe; they make videos about it, they write articles. Not just traveling, but also living alone, going out alone, exploring and experiencing things alone, going to a party alone, having fun alone. Basically, anything that could be done with friends, or should be. I'm exaggerating slightly, but I'm not so sure if I agree with it anymore, or if it was any of my intention to end up down the road all by myself. The circumstances had brought me to a point where I was the only one sitting by the window of an airplane; the whole row was empty.

If I must see things on the bright side, & keep a positive attitude, this solitude would define more independency; something that we're all looking for. You get to read another face of the story. Such as when you have to run the house all by yourself, cooking and cleaning would be on you, keeping it warm for the winter would be your responsibility, fixing the toilet when it doesn't flush; it's where you live, it cannot be abandoned. In the case of a lone traveler, the brain muscles flex when you need to reach the village in the left corner of nowhere. Somewhere so far, secluded; there are only two buses per week to the village. Or when you must wait in different stations for hours as your load feels to be heavier on the shoulders by the minute. The reward for all the hard work is to unpack, and slowly arrive onto the new land of your own.

Traveling has a mind of its own. Constantly being on the move takes quite a while to tune into. You lose, and then you find. You collect tokens, you leave things behind. You learn for yourself that simplicity is what makes it so pleasing. To dine with a hand-full of olives, green and black, a pear, & a slice of cheese. I too left things behind. A life, perhaps. The life itself would still be there, the premise was that I wouldn't be a part of it; it wasn't going to be my reality anymore. Time must've been the only thing that remained with me, as a close friend who kept shifting shapes wherever I went. Confusing, I wouldn't know how I should trust it, or make it work with every move. But, it was always there for me, sweet and sound, healing the wounds, rounding the sharp edges. Time, the moon, the sun with all their tricky games, the matter of the north and the south, as it always is, or the difference between this and that.

In the end, it's all alone all the while, not so sure how it could be fun.

We were much closer to the land. I hadn't been able to fully wake up yet. I squinted as I looked out the window. The trees were identifiable, they weren't just a mass of colors anymore.

Dark green, yellow, orange, a bit of red, & the sky that was completely blue; it was the middle of autumn, green wasn't the dominant color any longer. There were lands in between the forests, fields for different purposes that I wasn't quite sure what. And I saw lakes. So many of them.

We were at a distance where the houses and the roads still looked very petite. Even more adoring, they were as small toys that you could play with. The cars were driving down the streets, waiting at traffic lights here and there, with people who were probably going to work. I couldn't tell for sure what the local time was, but it was morning. As we landed, and I got to step in the hallways of the airport, I read the clock which was the same as my watch, it was only the sun that would rise and set differently.

Apparently, it was an odd season to visit the area, I discovered once I arrived. In fact, some of the locals wondered what I was doing there at that time of the year; I wasn't illuminated myself either. They kept saying that the winter was going to be dark, which I was technically familiar with, & had read about the concept, but in actuality, I was absolutely clueless. I was incapable of comprehending the extreme darkness they were speaking of. It is going to be dark, they said. I nodded, smiled, & told them that I understood; I don't think I did. Living in the darkness was a bit ironic too. We kept joking about it with Tina, a good friend that I met during the first journey. I was dreaming that time would show me its beautiful face. Only, life was noticeably getting dimmer and colder each day. Living in the darkness for a few months was only reality's big slap in the face to remind me that even dreams must be dreamt realistically. To be fair, my mind must've been fogged with all the bitter truths that being realistic was the last thing that occurred to me. I couldn't think straight ahead, no time to be worried about the darkness and very cold winter. The only clue was to move; things would be different anyway. However, I was not very far away from getting lost.

Thinking about it now, I find it all so naïve. How was I to know a thing about the future?! I was only sitting by the small window of an airplane, looking outside, trying to imagine how the airport looked like, how the officer at the passport control would react when they held my passport. They certainly would want to double-check my traveling documents; they had to make sure. I was daydreaming about the rest of the trip. I had a bus to catch. I wondered how the views would be like by the road, or if I'd meet a new friend along the way.

I yawned, looked at my face on the dark screen of Es-three, my dearly departed smartphone, to check how un-human I was: very! Nevertheless, I had no solution for fixing that, except that I spread another big yawn, rubbed my eyes for the sixteen thousandth time to wake up. I tricked myself by the promise of an afternoon nap, which would always work to get me up in the morning. I rolled up my sleeve to check the time, even though I couldn't tell if it was right.

Two Girls

I was sitting on the back seat of the car, leaning to the gray backpack behind me. Its strap was hanging loosely on my shoulders. The car stopped, I opened the door. It was the first trip on that car, and most probably the last. I had to look for the handle for a second. I thanked the two girls for the lift, wished them a nice vacation, told them I hope we would meet again somewhere; you'd never know about the future. I shut the door behind me.

It was a pleasant surprise that the bag was not heavy, quite the opposite, it was very light. There weren't so many things in it, just a couple pieces of clothes, six cans of beer, and some small stuff in the lid pocket. I wrapped the belt around my waist out of habit, & adjusted it on my shoulders. That was something that I loved about the gray bag, it would sit nicely on my back. Honestly, I didn't expect much of it. It was rather inexpensive as well, but it turned out to be such a great company. It was a perfect fit which is quite important when things get heavy. Oh, and it does get heavy, nineteen or over twenty kilograms. The weight should be distributed on the back evenly, otherwise, you wouldn't be able to keep it up for more than two minutes. It would still be painful to walk about, but at least the whole body would take an equal amount of pain, the shoulders, the back, the waist, and the knees, maybe even the souls of the feet.

Down the road, there was a construction, a shelter with a wooden board behind, & a sign picturing a bus. I passed it by, stood on a dry spot a few steps further away, and turned back around to face the road from the future; I would spot the cars before they reached me.

It was a sunny late winter's afternoon. It was not so cold, it wasn't warm either. The air was still. I was standing under the sun to enjoy it all even better, to produce some vitamin D under my skin. It had been a long dark winter, every beam of sunlight should've been absorbed. There wasn't much heat to the light, perhaps just a touch, it was too pale to get noticed. The sun wasn't so high above the horizon, it already wouldn't reach the middle of the sky on that day of the year; it was going to set soon. The shadows were tall. My shadow was blessed with the superpower of long legs; I could've arrived at the Cabin in two minutes walking in legs so tall. The road was narrow and straight, no turns until it disappeared down the horizon.

And the spot that I was standing by was beautiful; I was near the bus stop which provided enough space for a car to pull over.

The view of the road was really nice. Up the road, where the two girls dropped me, was the point where the road forked in three ways, so I could easily see the cars turning left towards me. I had more than enough time to raise my arm, hold my thumb up, & hopefully get a lift. The best part, however, was the sun; I had all the sun of that still afternoon. The sky was still clear; it was bright blue. Surprisingly, it had been clear the whole week. It must've been the kindness and generosity of the universe to grant us such pleasure after an enormous blizzard the week before. As was heard from the locals, it was the biggest snowstorm in the last one hundred years. The storm started late at night, it snowed for half a meter in about four hours. Very scary, isn't it?! It gets even scarier when you know that it was the first proper snow of the winter; it was the beginning of March. Our village, of course, got snowed in. The roads were blocked. The valley was silent, not even the slightest noise from the cars or buses full of curious tourists.

The morning after the blizzard was sunny. Not a single trace of the storm or the dark clouds whatsoever, as if it never even happened. We were left with a sparkly duvet of snow all throughout the land for as far as the eyes could see. A glorious morning, indeed.

I personally would've enjoyed it all better if Yasi, my friend who was visiting for a week, had made it to the Cabin before the blizzard. She literally arrived with the storm. Some might say she brought it with because her flight landed just as soon as the storm started. Therefore, she got stuck on the road in her small rental car. It snowed enough to block her way in just a couple of hours. Some trucks noticed her on their way back; they pulled the car out. She described it as "pouring snow", it was pouring down, she said over dinner, Hannah and Christine and I were sitting around the table. She survived, & nothing happened. A sunny week was her reward for going through such a nightmare. A bright clear sky with all the sun, & the privilege of the stars and the breathtaking northern lights.

I heard a car approaching from the distance. I looked up the road to see if it was coming in my direction. It was, so I slowly brought my thumb up, & put on a smile. A nice genuine smile is always very effective when you're asking strangers to give you a ride for free; I believe it goes a long way. At least, personal experiences have illuminated me with the fact. Live and learn, as they say. Not that I'm an expert on the subject. For some, it is considered a profession. But for me, hitchhiking is the last ticket to get somewhere, when there are no other options. I generally avoid it in the evenings, the darkness would make me uneasy. But then again, I would if I should. If I know, then, hitchhiking is a definite part of the trip, I make sure that it's done before the sun sets.

The car passed me by at a high speed, without the slightest sign of hesitation to stop.

The road was empty, the area seemed to be secluded. I prepared myself to be there for a long while, mentally and physically. It's usually a great help to hitchhike with a friend, for some reason, it creates a more trusting image. For some drivers, you wouldn't even exist, as if there's nothing on the side of the road, why bother taking a glance?! Hard to imagine the reason why. Sometimes the car would be too full of stuff. I'd like to think they're in such a great rush, & they must be somewhere so urgently that they cannot stop for you. They might be too concentrated on driving that they wouldn't be able to see anything but the road. Who knows maybe they're being judgmental. It's a broad investigation, examinations must be done. It might be regarding where they'd grown up, who their parents were or how they were being raised, the number of the siblings, father's income, or how much was given to them as their pocket money. But, in the end, I wouldn't know the rules; there are no rules when it comes to humans.

Can't tell if it's only a myth that two girls get a lift much quicker. It might not be true, but that's a common saying. I could actually see how it could be true. Females look safer.

There's a lower chance of getting robbed, or killed by a woman. Men have already built a reputation for themselves on that over the past few decades. At least, women look more trustworthy. Or perhaps it would be more entertaining for the male drivers to give a ride to the females because of the attraction between the two. I have noticed that female drivers tend to care less about the hitchhikers, which could as well be for the sense of security. Not always, however; I've met very interesting lady drivers. At any rate, official studies and statistics need to be checked before making any statements; I'm only curious. I guess any driver would give you a lift if they've hitchhiked before, if they understand the pain of not having a vehicle, & having to go to places on foot.

I stood still, my thumb ready to hold up as the question mark; I waited for a kind stranger to take me. Watching people becomes a source of entertainment if the wait is long. The boredom diminishes as I get myself busy with a small thought. I tried to remember the last time I officially hitchhiked. Not so sure, but I remembered a man who gave us a bag of plums fresh from his garden; Didam and I were traveling.

Speaking of which, I pulled Es-three out of my pocket to take a picture of myself for Didam, having the empty road behind me. As I was connected to the network later during the day to send her the photograph, I found out that we were hitchhiking at the same time, more or less, only, along with other roads, and different directions.

Nothing was happening. As was anticipated. I stood there for a while without getting a positive response. A few cars passed, none stopped. Some drivers motioned different moves with their hands, saying that they will soon take a turn to one of the very small villages. Some gave me a smile, & waved back when I said hello and goodbye. And some others had no reactions. I wondered what was going on in their cars, which radio channel they were listening to, how come they didn't care at all. And then again, the road was empty.

I was curious to see where I was. I could loosely locate myself on the map, but I was interested to see how the valley was like, the trees and the bushes, where the center of the village was, and the particular point where the sun was going to set. Would've been nice to take a walk around, but there wasn't enough time. Mount Hekla was out of sight, however, I was very close to reach the view, probably another turn or two down the road. It looked marvelous from the windows of our Cabin. As far as I'd learned, it was always a good sign to be able to see it. It meant that it was sunny, & the sky was mostly clear. It meant that I was rather close to the Cabin. It would be on my right side during my early morning runs down the road, then left as I'd return. Twenty minutes on the way go, & interestingly, fifteen minutes on the way back.

Taking our beautiful mountain as the point of reference, I tracked the sunrise during the runs, if it wasn't cloudy of course. The winter was coming to end, and the sun would glide to the side slightly, so each day would be longer than the day before, even by only two minutes. It was such an empowering figure to have out the window, the glorious mountain beyond the lake; it really was a queen. Alda called her the queen once, so the phrase stuck with me. Alda is one of the owners of the Cabin, alongside Kristin and Jon. She was talking about the view during one of our afternoon tea parties. She was describing what was in the area, the highlands beyond the hill right behind our Cabin. The queen, however, held another face. Intriguing, perhaps a bit scary too. I guess that's why she's the queen, not a frisky princess. There's something to up her game one head and neck above the rest. She was more than just a magnifying mountain; the power she was holding was rather intimidating. A massive eruption had been anticipated for a few years already; she was about to blow off some steam. And it was going to be a catastrophe right before our eyes; we had her as our great view out the window. If anything had to happen while I lived there, we could've watched the whole scenery, like a show or a live performance. Not that it would be fun to watch such a disaster; the notion of safe had to be modified according to the occasion. However, it would most certainly be an interesting event added to the set, even if you wouldn't survive in the end.

As Alda was telling more about the hypothetical situation, I couldn't help thinking about the tourists, & whether they'd plan their vacation differently if they knew all the things that I was hearing from a local. Would they still visit the country, I wondered and asked aloud. Who knows, the queen might never flare, a good trip would be missed in the end. The funny thing was that our queen wasn't the only one on the edge of a major explosion. There was a king not so far from her which would do more damages if he ever decided to cough or sneeze.

I wondered if I should walk down the road till I could have the queen in the sight, perhaps to feel more secure that I wasn't really too far away. Even if I wasn't able to catch a ride by the end of the day, which was one of the least possibilities, I would be able to get back by simply walking down the road as long as I had her on my side. It would only be a matter of walking, then, & walking only. I was still very far away, and it would've been a very long walk, but rather reassuring to know that I had more than one option. It was a silly idea anyway. I was only entertaining myself because getting a lift seemed to be a bit more challenging considering the circumstances. The empty road in a valley of nowhere, drivers with huge cars, & winter jet skis attached to the top, shouting that they were on their way to enjoy a pleasant weekend. Drivers who seemed to be occupied with their own world that wouldn't let them see much on the outside, & notice another human standing on the side of the road with a gray backpack. Not that I'm complaining, I was only standing without getting any response. At least some of them were kind enough to answer with a smile.

It was starting to get boring. I felt like drinking a beer, but I didn't; I don't believe it would look decent for a hitchhiker to be holding a can of beer in hand. I was supposed to be reflecting a trustworthy face of myself, to make the strangers feel comfortable to have me along; I don't believe drinking beer would be supporting the image. Some might find a casual beer in the afternoon to be cool, others might judge you for that. I couldn't risk it, really. The key point was to look as neutral as one could, blend it, & move on. Although, I did light a small cigar, one of those very small ones that I used to pick up from the airport's duty-free shop. It didn't taste the best, maybe that's why I stopped buying them. It was amusing enough for the moment. I had done all kinds of mind games to keep my mind entertained: I'd counted the cars passing my way to get an average number per minute, I tried to reach number sixteen by making simple math problems using the numbers on the license plate. I'd read the letters in between the numbers, & tried to come up with funny names for my imaginary pet, plant, daughter and son. Most of the cars were modern and relatively new, some were off-road trucks with super gigantic tires to make them even more massive. And I saw too many rental cars, tourists following maps to reach the point where they thought they need to be. None of which stopped to take me with.

I turned around o face the sun. There were still a few hours left to the sunset, thankfully it wouldn't get dark in the afternoon anymore. The sun wouldn't move much above the horizon, so the sunlight would somehow be directly on the level of your eyes. It was ironic, I wouldn't know how to enjoy it, the sunlight would be very pleasant, but quite unbearable for the eyes, rather blinding even with the sunglasses on, in a way you'd wish for some clouds or a nice shade. But then the day wouldn't be as nice if the clouds showed up. It was a never-ending game. I tried to enjoy it the best I could, tomorrow would've been rainy or snowy, you could never tell. The color of the sky had already started to change, I noticed. It was around that time of the day when the sunlight would turn golden, & would make everything look romantic, would make the countryside even more charming; I could've fallen in love then & there.

My small cigar was almost over, so I chucked it in the snow. I wondered what else I could've done to ease the wait. Nothing was moving on the empty road. I started humming a melody, perhaps one of the songs that we'd listened to in the car with Yasi earlier that day before she left to the airport. I tapped on the ground with the chunky soles of my boots to have a more pronounced base. I wondered if Yasi had made it on board, or if she was up in the air by then. She quickly disappeared up the highway after she dropped me off by an exit, where I could cross over to the other side and catch a ride back to the Cabin; she was in a great hurry. In about two hours, once I was connected to the network, I received her text message saying that she'd missed her flight.

After a couple minutes of humming and singing to myself with my unqualified voice, I decided it was best that I actually listened to some music. My music player was in the lid pocket of my backpack, exactly behind my head; I didn't even need to take down the bag to reach it. I plugged the earphones in my ears, pressed and held the play button to have the machine on. It started playing where it was left off. My music player didn't have a shuffle button, or any other features to play the songs randomly. I'd listened to the same playlist enough to know which song was coming up next: Enkh Jargal's Great Eagle Dance wasn't all that far away. I pushed the skip button. A few more cars passed, & I was presented the same reactions. I smiled, they smiled back. There it was, the music that I'd been craving for. I couldn't help but closing my eyes, and taking a deep breath; it's always a pleasure to listen to it. I dared to sing along, even though I didn't understand the words. I couldn't hear my ear-scratching voice through the earphones; I sang louder. I don't think I cared. Nobody was around, nothing but the crisp white snow, & an empty road.

It was hard not to move my head around from side to side, let my hips spring up and down lightly with the beat, and my shoulders to move along. I wasn't dancing, but I wasn't standing still either. Just as if you're walking, taking a step forward and back, but not really moving anywhere. My brain was getting quite out of itself. Closed my eyes again, lifted my head. I kept my arm and thump up in case a car passed by as long as my eyes were closed; I wouldn't want to miss a potential lift. But at the same time, I really didn't care, one minute less, or more.

The reality stopped before my eyes, not long, for only two seconds. Floating in between the images produced by my brain, I opened my eyes to catch myself dancing. The smile on my face was wide; the song was almost over. As I turned on my feet with the last notes of the song, I noticed a red car that had pulled over a few steps further; a young woman was behind the wheel.

Three Small Birds

The post office was closed when we arrived; it was past eight in the morning. Seemed to be true: it wasn't going to open. We didn't want to believe that, so we parked the car to wait. We asked the shopkeepers and storeowners nearby if they knew about the situation of the post office on that particular day, but they declared their cluelessness honestly. It might open, it might not. It would depend on the manager if he felt like working that day. It was a half-holiday on a summer's morning, in between the weekend and a long holiday; it was Monday. Any public department must be providing services until noon, but it was hard to tell in such circumstances. It seemed highly unlikely for any business to run, public or private, except for cafés and restaurants, or anything related to the beloved tourists.

We were very hopeful about the post office for some desperate reason, believed that soon they would open the doors. Perhaps by nine o'clock since it was such a special day. Some letters had to be sent before we could return back to the campsite down the valley, perhaps sleep a bit, freshen up. And eventually come across another party in the evening by the beach, or in the forest, or wherever the party crew fancied. The idea of sleeping was madly sweet; it was all I could think of. I know myself better though, no sleep falls upon my eyes before noon. Thankfully, I wasn't hungry anymore, the image of food was out of the mind. We'd decided we'd better eat in order to function a bit more normally. The brain operates abnormally when it hasn't gotten any rest in the past twenty-four hours. Food somehow becomes the main source of energy to keep the system running.

We spotted a small café across the avenue before turning into the driveway of the post office. It looked very local. Rather comforting to see a couple of older ladies working in front of the café. They were sitting by the non-stick oval pan, rolling the phyllo dough super thinly, spreading the filling in the center, and folding them neatly into squares. They would set their crafts aside to grill when an order came. They did it so effortlessly that you'd think anyone could do it, flipping the bread on the smoking hot griddle, brushing it with melted butter or oil as the dough was getting cooked and crisp; you would only treasure the skill for that very simple act if you ever tried making one for yourself.

I don't remember clearly, I was very tired, but I don't think we ordered any of that filled bread; we were considering it, but we switched directions. Instead, we had Menemen. It must be the best food for breakfast, even, some kind of an early lunch. I don't really prefer it for dinner, it's rather depressing once it's past three in the afternoon; it feels to be more like a day-time meal. It's a very simple dish, but the recipe may vary depending on who the cook is, which middle of what east they're from. Ours contained the perfect ratio of eggs and tomatoes. It also had the right amount of green pepper. The bell pepper shouldn't be too over-powering, in my opinion, it should be just about enough to give it a distinct bitterness. If I was cooking it at home, I would add some garlic as the onions were being fried, or after the tomatoes were cooked off. And I would fry the onions a bit more, maybe even until the edges were slightly burned, for the extra bittersweet among all the colors and flavors.

I ordered mine with three eggs; it was a three-egg kind of day. Normally, two eggs would be just about enough, boiled or fried in butter, but it wasn't really an ordinary day. If I was making the food myself, I wouldn't break the yolks into the mixture. I would've let them cook for a few minutes after I scrambled the whites with the rest of the concoction. I might even put the lid on for a minute to have the yolks in my desired consistency, creamy yet runny, but certainly not raw. And as the dish comes to the table, I would first eat the other parts of the food. I would keep the golden yolks intact till the end of the meal where I would finally sprinkle some coarse salt on top, & would put the whole yolk inside my mouth one by one; what you eat the last matters. There's no greater pleasure than to have the yolk melt in the mouth slowly as the flakes of salt kicks random spots in the mouth. Eggs cry out for salt, are best friends with black pepper, & chives and parsley are always welcomed in the party.

I asked the waiter to only use sucuk in my dish; I don't care much about sausage in Menemen. I wasn't expecting such a café to use a high-quality sausage either. It wouldn't add much to the dish in terms of nutritional values, taste, or texture. Sucuk, on the other hand, could be a nice touch. It's still processed meat, but a very flavorful one, jam-packed with spices and tasty animal fat. It was a satisfying dish. The after taste remained in my mouth was so strikingly pleasing that I didn't dare spoil it with anything else.

The whole café, the waiters and the waitresses, the chef and the ladies by the fire gave me the impression that the food was coming from their village. Rosemary from the bushes in front of their door, garlic and onion of their own garden. The three eggs taken from the chicks in the yard, which, if given enough time, would turn into three small birds. But, it was downtown; things were obviously bought from a supermarket.

The stomachs were full. All left to do was to wait for the post office to open if it ever would, which never really did. A power nap would've been the perfect pudding following the luscious breakfast we just had. But, knowing that I wasn't going to fall asleep, I didn't even bother. I saved the nap for the afternoon by the beach, once we were back in the forest: the very welcoming society of trees. I closed my eyes, I could at least give them a rest. Random images of what might've potentially happened to the rest of the day flashed before my eyes. I thought of going for a swim in the salty water. I would then fall asleep on the sands under the sun; the sound of the waves would only be my silicone brush to sweep the beat of the hard techno music off my brain. Waiting for the post office with an open-end could be such a bore, however, it was rather nice to be away from the party wolves even for a few hours, people who lived in a village where the only concern was how to party, and where.

I had been starting my days with a swim the whole time I was camping in the valley. It was only natural to crave for a morning dip physically, not just psychologically. From what I was seeing out the windshield, there was a glowing blue sea on the other side of the avenue, calling for a slow dive; set aside the reality this once. The waves were appealing, the sparkles of the sands seemed to be delightful. I don't think there would be a better way to start the day, other than floating weightlessly in the lukewarm salty water. To have an oblivion moment in the gentle heat of the early morning sun, under the quiet breeze sailing through the skin. There wouldn't be much to worry about as long as the sun shines, as long as it's summer.

It's a dull observation, but summer's getting shorter each year. It might as well be my personal perception, the fact that time feels different as you get older. Regardless, I do believe seasons have started to schedule another timetable. Just as soon as you begin to appreciate the colors of the autumn, the temperature drops significantly, & the wintery clouds hide the sun away. Soon, it gets far colder to be enjoying the day outdoors. The snow is highly unpredictable these days too, one year it's a lot, and the next year it's too little to turn things into a crisis. The most unusual is when it snows by the end of March. The spring is not really springy anymore; it's just a warmer version of winter. It is merely a few weeks of confusing weather, cold blasts along with gusty winds. Summer comes as a surprise, you can never be so sure about its arrival. Some years it strikes in late April, otherwise, it doesn't come until the middle of August. However wrong the timing might be, it's always nice to have summer; to be as carefree and light and cheerful as a day at the beach. My very small daypack was more than enough to make the day into the night; it was black, would fold in on itself to become as small as a pack of tissues. The perfect vehicle which would provide enough room to carry a bottle of water, a small wallet with a bit of money to secure the comfort, and some sunscreen for extra protection. A light jacket wouldn't be a bad idea for the evening; it could simply be hung from the side of the bag. And a smartphone, which I gradually and eventually learned how to live without. You can be wearing your swimsuit, the sunglasses wouldn't really need to leave your face.

 Not much to worry about, things are always fine in summer. It doesn't last very long anymore; the wind was already much cooler, & the drop of the temperature even by a couple degrees wrung out the cheer of the morning; it was only September. The lucky thing was that the sun was still hot. My theories could all be false. The world could be living on as normally as it ever did. And I was only presuming these because of my bad timing, when I was where I was. Perhaps I was only living things on the opposite side of the cycle; things needed to be shifted.

I closed my eyes for a few seconds to check if there was any sleep in the background; none that I could reach. The sun was up, which made me feel like I needed to be up as well; otherwise the day would be trashed. I leaned my head up against my seat, looked up the rooftop window. The sun was on its way to reach the middle of the bright blue sky. There was a small piece of cloud floating in my frame; it made the whole view so dreamy. The small cloud was getting into all kinds of forms as the wind blew, I could see the whole world in it. I blinked, watched it shift shapes, I blinked again. There was no sleep in my land, so I might as well take advantage of the given time. That was the ultimate idea behind all of it, to take advantage and make the best of anything that's been given, and try to enjoy it the most. It's a saying that we used to joke with Soheil, my brother, & friends of that episode. The idea became very appealing to me. So much that it easily could've been the motto; why not?!

The doors of the post office were still closed, the streets were just as quiet. I was so surprised to see the neighborhood so empty, which made me wonder where all the tourists and visitors were. The question answered itself just as I took a look at the watch on my left wrist: it was still very early. The sun seemed to be rotating in the sky quickly, I noticed, the shadows were shrinking; the car would soon be fully exposed to the sun. How unbearable the inside of the car would get once the sun was above us. The heat felt to be getting closer. My door was open, so were the rest of the windows. The air was floating softly inside the car, I'm afraid it wasn't nearly enough. The heat was too intense for the early hours of the morning.

The small grass field by the post office looked very inviting. I could've laid there to rest the body, the feet, and the eyes. More appealing than the grass was the turquoise sea beyond the avenue. It wasn't very far, only a few hundred steps away. I could've walked there, dipped my feet in the water in less than five minutes. I was tempted, though I couldn't make sure if the avenue was lined with any fences. There weren't any traffic lights for as far as I could see, so there had to be some blockage between the road and the sea; there usually is around the area for safety reasons. It made me rethink the beach plan, whether or not it was worth the trouble. I couldn't imagine myself walking up or down the avenue to find a green light. Or, if I had to skip the traffic light, I would have to cross over the fences. With the extreme exhaustion of mine, I needed bolder motivations. The beach might be different than the image it was reflecting from the distance. It might be full of sharp rocks, not even suitable for dipping the feet in. I didn't want to go through all that only to find something far beyond my anticipations. The sea looked magical from where I was sitting, all I could ever fancy at the moment. I didn't dare to spoil the sweet image. I had already been disappointed more than my capacity in the last couple months that I don't think it would've been healthy to push my limits any further. I couldn't let myself down with my own hands and arms and legs, not my own will.

It was the beginning of a lesson; whether or not I learned anything is questionable. Plans change, paths take different turns. They become pictures from the past that never took place in reality; merely an imagination in the head. It felt like living in a parallel universe. One small change in the flow of incidents, & I was elsewhere. It was a new stage that I was facing. For most of it, I would end up in places that I wasn't supposed to be, & I most certainly did not expect. Looking back at things, most of what happened, or have been done was never any of my intentions; they weren't a part of the plan. Plan! Sounds funny, in a way. How naïve of me to actually make plans, imagining, even if it's for a very brief moment, that the future could be fabricated. Who are we to map the future?! As if it's up to us to determine it. Various forces influence the execution of an idea, and the way we come up with a decision, we simply wouldn't know what. I'm not talking about planning to get a cup of coffee with friends at the gas station near the house, or go grocery shopping for a special dinner party. More serious ones. Entering another country, for instance. You would think that it should be easy: get a ticket, hop on a plane, or train, or bus. Start cycling on your bike if the money is not enough, walk, or even swim if there's a body of water anywhere. It's more complicated than that, I would say, think again. It depends on higher authorities to let you leave the country, or enter in. The strict bureaucracy in on the way, rules, stamps and signatures. There's a point where people become invisible. Humans turn into numbers, documents, & pieces of paper. Names don't have any meanings anymore, they're just a bunch of letters. As long as they don't approve of you, your conditions, and most probably your bank account, you're not allowed to make a move. Technically, you're trapped.

In my case, inside a car in front of the main post office of the town, watching the blue sea with white foamy waves that would brush the yellow sands. I was busy taking notes of the colors of the sky which is not always blue. I was thinking about the land on the other side of the sea, not so far away from us; we could reach it by a simple ferry. It sounded funny in my head that I wasn't allowed to visit, even if it was for a quick drink. A fish would, a seagull could. But not us. Plants and trees are out of this game, they're a bit different. They need the Earth, the soil, & the ground; they have roots. Humans roots too. But, we can manage them to survive. We can replant if we're smart enough. If the environment is not suitable, if things are not well-considered, the roots unbind; we would stop growing. Soon enough we'd die too. We are born with something called freedom, the ability to think, which is supposed to make us different than the rest. It's tricky to acknowledge the freedom, it comes in many faces. I was free, at least, I could see that. At that moment, I was the freest person I could think of. No jobs to get me up in the morning, no children to tie me down, yet, that was the best I could improvise: waiting in the car under the heat of the late-summer sun, embracing every drop of sweat, for I was aware that summer was too short to complain.

Regardless, none of it was all that unexpected. The road is always full of surprises, I was already familiar with the view. It may turn at any moment; you should turn with it if you don't want to crash down the valley. I was well-prepared, so were my bags. It was only the tension of the paperwork that wouldn't leave much space for happiness. It may make you forget that it was the ultimate goal, to be able to enjoy any given moment. I would catch myself mad at life every so often, cringed in a corner with a tough frown in the middle of my forehead before I could remember that life is nothing but moments. These moments. A deep breath in, & I would open my eyes to the new world, feeling like a stranger in a new land. Even a foreigner to myself for most of the cases. My reactions would be different, my choices would be unknown. I'd allow myself to do as I wished; it was my parallel universe after all. It could always be one of those exams that life put you through, to test out if you've learned enough so far. It was a pretty hard one, in a way, it was going to take me a while to find myself back again.

I was getting lost somewhere, I should've seen it coming. I was looking, but not enough recognizable features were found to make me the person I was. Routines and habits were left behind, friends and family were elsewhere, & I couldn't relate to what was around. I felt like nothing but a name, & a hand-full of belonging to be identified with, clothes, pens and notebooks that I fit in my bags to carry along wherever I went.

I took a big sip out of my blue bottle of water which was almost empty. I put the bottle back in the small day-pack, & slide it down by my feet. I scooched more to my left to avoid the direct sunlight which was more than halfway inside the car. It was getting unbearably hot. I wondered how come the post office wasn't opening. It was the perfect moment to dive into an existential crisis. I filled my lungs with the mind-numbing hot wind that was blowing in my face. I was too tired that every thought seemed depressing; I exhaled slowly. Keeping a healthy distance off my concerns seemed to be the easiest way to get them fixed for the moment. Things do look smaller when you get away, not all that terrifying anymore. A huge rock along the path would seem like a small stone, perhaps a grain of sand from afar.

I was following a path that I had drawn, which would ideally lead me toward some kind of happiness that I was dreaming of. But, in reality, the path was so vague that you could barely call it so. It's not really a path unless you walk along back and forth for at least a few times; the ground needs to remember your footsteps. It's only a passage otherwise. The footsteps quickly disappear if you pass it by once or twice, either it's on the snow, dirt, or grasses of a meadow. And it's only after the first time that you actually begin to notice the surrounding, what's around the path you were walking by since you're not just watching your footsteps anymore, careful not fall down, step on a rock, stumble upon a piece wood that once belonged to a tree, or some beautiful flowers that have recently bloomed. You get the chance to look up, get to observe what else is there.

I had only drawn a line to connect the two dots together, where I was and the happiness that I was seeking for. The line was passing by places beyond my usual way, so I got to ramble about, explore the other side of the yard over the fences. And in the end, there I was, beyond anything that I ever imagined; in a hot car parked in front of the post office, overlooking the bluest sea. Nobody was expecting anything from me, nothing was waiting for me either, except for my gray bag in the village amongst the woods; that was my only concern.

It was fairly disturbing to wait so, let's be honest here. Waiting wasn't a constant act, however, it was an on-going task in the back of my mind. Every minute would pass by with a certain expectation. It might be as small as starring at the door of the post office to open. It could be a great deal such as purchasing the aeroplane ticket to leave the country; you just wouldn't know when. Constantly waiting for a message, a phone call, or a response to your electronic note to let you know that you're finally permitted to book your flight. I kept asking myself if it was finally the day. Tomorrow morning?! Perhaps the message would arrive by the end of the week? Or the beginning of the next week? And the weeks stretched into months. Time had started to feel different, slower, or a bit longer. It left me in a limbo, an empty space where things were rather senseless. I was waiting, so I couldn't go far. I couldn't remain still either for it seemed to be a waste of time. The disturbing part was the uncertainty of the length of the wait. You're waiting for a bus, let's say, & you know the exact hour of its arrival. If you're late, you would run in order to get yourself to the stop. If you're early, on the other hand, you might visit a shop for an ice-cream, or a café for steaming coffee if it's a cold winter's day, or tea if coffee is not your type of drink. Perhaps you take a moment to look at the crown of the trees, how the leaves swing about with the wind, the birds, & the people who are walking along with you. But the plot would lead another line when you don't know when the bus would arrive. What would you, then?! Getting a cup of coffee would seem like a huge risk.

The sensation of waiting for the post office to open wasn't all that different from the everyday life that I was living then. Every thought and every action was stained; things were sifted through. As if my hands were all tied up, & I was left at the beach. The sea would still be stunning, & the warm sands would still feel delightful to take a nap on. I was still able to dip into the water, but swimming was not an option. The thought of drowning might keep me away.

I'd rather believe that the universe was trying to teach me a lesson there, to be able to see things on the bright side in the future. To be more patient, give things a change so they'd happen on their own. The circumstances drenched out my ability to see the beauty in ordinary life. All I had to do was to look above, there lies the sky which is known to be ours. The land was getting more and more complicated, but what about the sky?! I wondered who could touch it.

    I finished the water; the blue bottle was all empty. It was a hot morning, even though the summer heat had already peaked. I kept my eyes on the sky. I wasn't keeping track of time, so I wouldn't know for how long I remained so. It was satisfying to watch the passage of the clouds, try to identify their shapes. I followed the white line left by an airplane, & kept starring at it till it vanished away.

Platform Number Four

The bus finally arrived at the platform. For some obscure reason, I'd assumed that it would arrive at platform number four. The whole station was smaller than our School; I was only a few steps away from the right platform. I had sensed something off about platform number four. I had to make sure; I couldn't risk it. I asked the lady at the ticket office. She explained, but I could not understand. A guy who was standing close enough to hear our conversation told me platform number four wasn't the correct one for my destination. I obviously didn't understand him either; we were speaking the language of no-language. He walked me to the last platform; it was platform number nine.

The bus was old, similar to our school bus back in primary school. I was the first one to get on board, not that there were so many people queuing. I showed the address to the driver to be safe that it was the bus I was supposed to be on, & to let him know where I needed to get off because I clearly had no idea. He nodded. I read his eyes behind his sunglasses that it was the right bus after all; I could comfortably take my seat.

I got to pick where to sit, which, most obviously, wouldn't be any other one than the first row. I wanted to have a broad view of the road, to fully witness where I was going. I put the dancing rucksack by the window, & sat by the aisle. My right arm had a place to rest; the rucksack had been such great support all the way through. The window in front of me was wide open, even though at that point I could only see the gray walls and metal seats of the coach station, glass doors, & passengers walking by; my imagination promised neat scenery. Only a few more minutes till we could leave the platform to be precise on the bus schedule.

By that point, I had already stopped wondering about the suitcase, the small brown suitcase; it went missing in between the flights, got lost somewhere along the way. To be honest, I was slightly relieved that I didn't have to carry it with me all the way to some village in the valley of nowhere; it was only the rucksack on my shoulders, and now, sitting under my arm. Who knew where the suitcase really was by then?! Standing quietly in a dark corner of an airport. It was a disappointment not to greet it back again around the luggage ring at the final airport. The ring turned and turned, and turned, and nothing came up under my possession; no trace of a small brown suitcase with a blue belt wrapped around it. I took a walk around the ring once it stopped; I had to be certain it was actually happening to me before I could laugh out loud at the ridiculousness of the situation, & eventually find a way to fix it. I wasn't worried, it was just funny. I had heard stories of the suitcases going missing mysteriously, & never showing up at the final destination. But in the end, they were dispatched to the travelers safe and sound. In fact, they were delivered to their door in one piece. And according to those stories, I knew that I had to file a report before I left the airport. I would lose all my privileges as soon as I stepped out, and nobody would take any responsibility in any way.

I followed the signs to reach the lost and found department in one of the aisles behind the duty-free shops. It was a wide room, the front wall was glass. I knocked on the open glass door, & let myself in after a few seconds of not getting any attention. I was in a hurry, I had two other buses to catch, & I wasn't looking forward to missing either one of them. The service agent asked me to have a seat as soon as he was done with the previous client. We greeted each other in a polite but friendly manner. He offered me a drink, I asked for some water.

We took a tour around the luggage delivery ring to investigate the situation personally. He wrote down some notes on papers attached to his clipboard, checked a few boxes on the list, flipped a couple pages; we returned to his office. He assured the delivery of the suitcase back to my door, told me there was nothing to worry about. He said that it was rather common, & it happened often. They would bring it to me wherever I was, even if it was the other corner of nowhere.

I smiled. My only concern was for the next couple of days, what I was going to wear, or how I was supposed to keep busy. I took a sip of water in the plastic cup I was holding, tried to run through the items that I'd manage to squeeze in the suitcase. I couldn't remember much, I'd packed in such a great hurry that it was impossible to think twice before I fit them in the luggage. Within the next few months, I realized I had everything I'd ever need, maybe even more.

The agent handed me a form to fill, & a couple papers to sign. They were about my identity and my suitcase's: what the suitcase looked like, what type of luggage it was. If it was a backpack, or a duffel bag, similar to what RJ had chosen as his vessel. RJ was a friend that I met later in the afternoon, a couple hours after I arrived at the School. His life was surprisingly similar to mine, only, he'd picked a duffel bag, & I'd decided to take the brown suitcase.

    I had to identify the suitcase on the list: hard-case, plastic, or metal. Mine was coated with fabric, in the color of brown, warm with earthy tones. It was only a wheeled carry-on, but it could magically hold the whole universe, I'm not even exaggerating. I was quite confident with all my answers. I knew the suitcase too well; it had been with me for ten years already by then. My mother had bought it for me before I left them. I was going through all the questions quickly. However, my brain froze when I had to write down the name of the brand, the small title carved on the top left corner of the front pocket. Or, was it right?! I couldn't recall the name. That was shocking, and very embarrassing. Names are hard work, they're not my field of expertise, but it was unbelievable how I could not remember that one. I knew it, of course I did! Although, at that moment, I doubted myself if I ever read the name at all, or simply gave it an empty look, & went through the letters carelessly. No, I certainly knew the name, I just couldn't recall it.

    I raised my head off the papers in front of me, looked at the agent with a wide smile on my face because it was so stupidly funny. Different combinations of letters and random words were crossing the back of my eyes. Some names were landing on the tip of my tongue to speak it out loud, but not quite; not quite. Poor suitcase, it's been with me for over a decade, it most certainly deserved better than that. It had bravely carried my stuff in every move, from one flat to another, one apartment to the next, which would happen quite often. It never left me alone during the trips and travels, & I ingloriously couldn't remember the name. The agent was such a wonderful person, he smiled kindly once he found out why I was so puzzled. He said that it was okay, my boarding pass was enough information to track it down; the rest was paperwork. But he could obviously see how and why it was all very funny. I mentioned that there was a blue belt wrapped around the suitcase. That should make it one of a kind, not that it wasn't already, but at least its uniqueness would help me feel a bit less guilty about not remembering its beautiful name.

The engine of the bus started to run; the driver was getting ready to leave the platform in a couple of minutes. The bus was rather empty, and the very few people on board were old folks. It was a sunny afternoon, very hot considering that it was the middle of autumn. Fairly warm weather for the southern regions was quite expected, but not sweating hot. I could've darkened my skin color by a couple degrees if I took a nap under the direct sunlight. The heat was a sweet reminder of the summer, just as light, perhaps even lighter now that the suitcase was missing.

Long hours of traveling, & not sleeping throughout the night had left me with nothing but enormous fatigue. Although, I had taken quite a lot of naps on the way. Basically, whenever an opportunity arose I would shut my eyes to drown in a shallow sleep. Technically, I've had a good amount of sleep, but the only thing that could freshen me up, & make me human again was a good night's sleep; not even a thousand naps could ever take the place of that.

The bus took a brief tour around the boulevard which was running alongside the river, made a few stops to pick up other passengers, & finally joined the road to leave the town. I appreciated the serenity, was glad the trip was eventually off the highway. Highways and main roads can also hold so many interesting attractions, especially if it's the first ride, or the second, only, not as jaw-dropping as the side paths.

The river was running down through the hills and cliffs covered in trees. It was wider than what I'd seen on the digital map. Might as well be deeper than what I'd pictured. The road was curling by the river, every twist was a subtle surprise. I saw villages here and there, houses detached from the crowd which seemed to be leading their own lives amongst the woods. I saw the vineyards, olive trees which I couldn't tell if the fruit was black or green from the distance. By the houses, there were ropes holding wet clothes soon to be dry. With an intense sun as such, they would fully dry in a couple of hours. Even during the coldest months, as long as it was sunny, it wouldn't take long for the clothes to be back in the closet. The sun was even more intense further down in the south where I got to live for a few months during the winter. Even though there were only a couple hundred kilometers in between the two villages, the weather shifted drastically. I moved back up north in the middle of the winter. From dry-cold, all of a sudden it was wet-cold. Rainy winter was quite new; I've never had a snowless winter before. The following year, as I heard from my friend Roham, was apparently quite nice and warm. A rather springy-winter. My timing took me to its most bizarre condition, just like the blizzard incident at the Cabin, & the forest fire which I'll be telling you about in a moment.

You see, somehow, for the catastrophic fires only, I couldn't complain about the constant rain. The dark clouds that almost never cleared. The jackets wet from the mad rain, damp feet, and a runny nose. It was only fair for the land to have the wettest winter after all the woods that burnt earlier in the year. Not so sure if I was lucky to witness one of the major fires which occurred only a couple days after my arrival. Our neighboring valleys were mostly burnt. The forests that I was passing by on the bus at that moment were gone in less than a hundred hours. I was on my way to a village, riding happily to someplace known as the School. The stunning scenery surrounding the road was missed by falling in for another short sleep. The bus sailed into the woods, gifted me the view for the first and the last time. And I was snoozing. Would I have done differently if I knew a thing about the future? How was I to know about the fire around the corner?! Too tired to keep awake, I was fully exposed to the softest sun of an autumn afternoon which was not at all helping me stay up. It was the road to the village, I must've said to myself, & would've assumed I'd pass it by for so many more times since the plan was to stay for a while. I can always see it, even during different seasons in different coatings and colors. How was I to know that they were going to turn black?! I wouldn't look away for a split second. I would've locked my eyes on them, no blinking, just watching the heavenly scene out the window. To be fair, my eyelids were pleasantly heavy by such a charming road, so napping wasn't such a bad idea after all.

It was actually not a very long nap, perhaps about four minutes or so. The signs of a small town not so far away started to appear just so gradually. I took off my sunglasses, rubbed the nap off my face, & put the shades back on; the sun was too bright for the sleepy eyes. The bus took a turn into a small town with very narrow alleys. I was concerned for a second for a potential unfortunate accident, but then I remembered that the driver probably drove that route at least a couple times a day, for how many years; he could've driven with his eyes closed. So, I enjoyed watching the town, the small playground in front of the church, cafés and shops, & I enjoyed it the best. Later, I found out about a bar next to that café, & another bar behind one of those alleys, which I never really learned the directions to. And because it was my first time there, I missed the gas station in the corner, & the supermarket in front of it. I was amazed by the stone houses, people who were having a pleasing afternoon, and the sound of their conversations that I couldn't understand. Regardless of the beauty I was blessed with, I was eager to arrive already. The ride was taking longer than I'd expected. Things were new, the road would certainly feel longer on the first trip, but other than that, the bus had to make so many stops in different corners of the towns and villages, & I was too tired for that. I didn't bother checking my map, but calculating the matter on my watch, I could tell that we were close; I would expect the driver to turn to me at one of these stops, tell me we were there at last.

We were back on the road again, turning left and right with it, proceeding to our destination. Pretty soon, we arrived in a bigger town. I was sitting on the edge of my seat, knowing that my stop was there for sure. Well, we were close, but not quite there yet.

We reached our town, & the village would be about four kilometers away. The bus took a big tour; I was watching with the utmost curiosity. I was aware that I was missing many details, things that I couldn't know even existed. But I was all eyes and ears to absorb the most I can, perhaps a bit of nose too. I couldn't even locate the river, but I knew it was on the side somewhere. I was exhausted, however, & indeed impatient to finally be in the village; I had been waiting for months already. We were now heading toward the woods, slowly leaving the town behind. I still hadn't heard from the driver. Disappointing, I thought maybe he'd forgotten me, though I was only a couple steps away from him. We passed by Alvaro's, & the Pizzeria. I was resting my chin on my arm on the pole in front of my seat, so I somehow managed to notice those two historical restaurants. Or perhaps it was my selective perception, the fact that I was getting hungry too; I couldn't remember when I ate what I ate. Those restaurants became our ultimate go-to, whether for casual gatherings, food, or drinks before we went out for the night. Mr. Pombalino, who owned a small café in the center of the town, would shut down the place around midnight, so Alvaro's would be our next stop. Alvaro would still keep the doors open for friends and family to drink more wine and chat, watch television, & put on some music occasionally to have a dance. If we were to stay out late, Alvaro's was our place. The Pizzeria was somewhere we would go for the actual food. It was a proper family restaurant. The food was quite good in both of them, let's be fair, but the menu was broader at the Pizzeria; Alvaro's was rather a café with a menu of a few different dishes. And, of course, the lunch menu that never went missing from the routine.

Even though the Pizzeria had a few pages of food to offer, I don't think I tried anything but the loin salad. That was the only food I would order whether for lunch or dinner. It somehow turned into a reaction as the waiter asked what I'd like to have. Rather, some type of joke amongst us; another funny joke Luís made, & I laughed out loud for a minute each time I heard it. One night, as he was joking about the salad, he realized that he had ordered the same pizza whenever we ate there; the joke only became funnier.

Although, I do believe I ordered another dish once. Naja and I had walked there for dinner. It was a couple weeks after I was back from the south. We decided to go to the bar down the road, a few minutes away from the gas station. A sandwich and a glass of wine was our perfect plan for dinner. The bar was closed. Since we were already out, halfway down the road to the town, we proposed the Pizzeria to treat ourselves with a nice proper dinner. Something comforting, warm and filling for the winter was getting tougher than expected. I was about to order my usual salad, but the cold took my eyes off the salad section. I started to seek other options. Or, perhaps it was Naja who encouraged me to try something other than the boring loin salad. Frankly speaking, it was a boring salad. It was a set of vegetables such as cucumber, red cabbage, tomato, lettuce, and sweet corn which I never really touched, with some slices of cold pork which played the role of the loin in the salad. And it was all topped with a drizzle of mayo-based dressing, tangy and sweet. The funny thing about the salad was that the components weren't even mixed. The food was a colorful combination of shredded vegetables placed side by side on a big white rimless plate. It looked nice, and probably was healthy enough to keep me going back to it again and again. It was also a hefty salad, I would be quite stuffed once I was done with it. Well, I have the habit of not leaving anything on my plate, unless it's sweet corn, not only because I can't be bothered with taking my leftover, but I strongly disagree with throwing away food, especially when it comes to meat. The heftiness of the salad, however, was almost nothing compared to the dinner I had with Naja. I don't exactly remember the name of the food, but it was something about stuffed pork cutlets fried till crispy on the outside, with some rice and a small simple salad on the side. And, obviously, wine, red wine; there was always red wine.

We were both quite full by the end of the meal, & a bit concerned about our return to the village. It was cold, perhaps one of the coldest nights of the winter. It wasn't a short walk either; the School was four kilometers away. The only solution that we could come up with to get us back faster was to hitchhike. We kept walking down the road, with the plan of raising the left arm up as soon as we'd hear a car approaching. It was only a minute or two after we started walking down the road where a car pulled over in the darkness a few steps away from us. Happy and excited about our instant success, we almost ran to the car. It was a police car, we realized just as we got closer. That was intimidating for a second, I never know where hitchhiking is illegal, the laws work differently in every country. Although, even if it was illegal, the two police officers were considerate and generous enough to give us a lift.

The bus passed by the infamous gas station, which I didn't notice for the extreme boredom, but I can now mention it because I know the gas station is there; it was our nearest coffee shop, in a way, the only one. It was our meeting point, someplace to shoot coffee, & take a break from the day. The bar down the road was technically within the territory of the village next-door. There was a local sports club by the church which would only be open during the weekends.

The bus roared up the hill, & took a sharp turn. The road was narrow, surrounded by the old shabby houses of the village. We reached up the hill to a rather wide flat parking space on the side. The driver slowed down by pushing the brake pedal; the bus screamed loudly. He stopped under the very old sign of a bus stop. My chin was still resting on my hands on the pole, looking out the wide windshield in front of me. I wondered why he stopped; there was nobody out there to stop for, neither was on the bus except for me. The driver turned around to look at me. He had a neat smile on, which could only mean one thing: we were finally there. I almost jumped off my seat for the excitement sizzling inside, thanked him a million times, & got off the bus.

There was an astonishing valley underneath my footsteps. My breath was taken away for a few moments, I found my way to the gate. It was an old metal gate. The fences and locks that had rusted effectively. Two sets of stairs welcomed me in opposite directions as I passed the gate; to the left, to the right. I held the straps of the black rucksack tightly, & watched my steps as I walked downstairs to the left. The stairs had diminished over the years, you had to watch out not to miss any steps, & roll down to the floor. The building itself looked rather old. The tall doors and windows on the tall walls would let you enter different rooms of the building. The doors were closed, though I wasn't really curious to see inside yet. I passed by the small front yard greeting me down the stairs, walked to the terrace to find out the world going on there; the view was uninterrupted. I stood still. There was another terrace almost identical to the left-hand terrace on the opposite side of the building. They both had a set of stairs which would lead you to the yard, where you could find blocks of the edible garden in a field of grass, with a hand-made black bench in the middle, a few trees. There were two football goals that were absolutely repurposed; one had turned into protected shelves for pots of plants and flowers, and the other one was garnished with ropes as washlines. I hadn't yet been able to blink.

The four o'clock sun was falling on half of the terrace, was lightening up the whole space. There was a mural on the wall, a woman washing the clothes; it had almost fully covered the wall. I appreciated it for a few seconds. There was also an L-shaped white couch in front of the painting in the middle of the terrace; they were both facing the beautiful valley. During the winter, Luís and Denisas decided to discard the couch for it was too ashy; the milky white color was rather gray after the snowing ashes of the forest fire. They also had to scrape off the mural for its time had come.

I put the bag on the corner of the couch, stood by the stone railings under the direct sunlight, & leaned against the column. Fantabulous, I didn't think about anything for seconds. I watched the village down the School with its church, the old giant chestnut tree by the road, the hills covered in green trees, & the windmills far away over the horizon. It was hard not to fall for it. I believe I kept watching for a minute before I could explore the right-hand terrace, the yard downstairs, the bathrooms, & all the rest. I took my time to appreciate it, & thank the universe to grant me with such beauty in the end; I had been waiting for so long.

It felt like heaven. Heaven in a dead-end. It usually takes me a while to understand what kind of dead-end I've landed on. It took me about a month to figure things out when I moved further down south. The first couple of days would usually be busy with exploring the village, or the town. Where to do the shopping, where to get a drink. Then comes exploring the paths, the main streets, the back alleys, short-cuts and long-cuts. It's always nice in the countryside, the air is fresh, you have the privilege to wake up to the sound of the sheep and the cows and the bells around their neck, the roosters, the loud chainsaw of the neighbors. Then it becomes clear that, physically speaking, it is going to be as far as it would get; the path doesn't go far beyond, & the town has ended. The world inside is endless, however. Getting to meet new friends, hear new stories of everyday lives, discovering whether they shake hands as they greet each other or if it's a gentle hug. The lunch menus of the local restaurants, how they keep warm in winter, or how they cool down during summer. I'd usually ask them about the town, how come so many people had left, or why the population is reduced in half.

A dead-end looks different from one village to another. Sometimes there's nothing, nothing at all. Only houses of the residents, barns, gardens and farmlands, and a beauty that has not been touched. A car would then become a key element to this living. A few months of such life and you realize something is seriously missing: where's everybody gone. Makes me wonder, once again, about the ones who stayed.

There's plenty more time in the countryside, no heavy traffic on the way to work, not much of a distraction. You should come up with your own materials as a source of entertainment to fill in the gaps. Perhaps it's then that the creativity blooms. Local festivals, small cultural gatherings, picking fruits off the trees. Collecting beautiful rocks along the path in the forest would become so entertaining that you start wondering how you could be missing such treasures all your life. After a certain amount of time, you'd finally learn how to laugh at the jokes of the new people, to an obscure sense of humor.

The remoteness of the village never stops fascinating me. Our village, I rephrase, anywhere that I had the privilege to call home, even for a very short while. I used to think about the seclusion, the isolation, emptiness, & peculiar loneliness. Made me wonder how they kept living there more than the reason why. The limited number of buses concerned me, decayed teeth and a mouth full of cavities. It was sad sometimes to see the children, the enormous energy going toward unintended directions. Villagers would be villagers, almost everywhere. The ones who are concerned about the late harvest, the dry lands, their houses that had been washed away with the flood, or burnt down by the fire. They need to worry if a worse catastrophe would be blooming the following year. Which would, in case you're wondering about the future.

And I do have a suitcase, I remembered as I was speaking with Johanna and Liudvika, who arrived back at the School in four or five minutes, most probably from a coffee break at the gas station. I greeted them loudly as they were walking down the stairs, as warm as the sun, as cheesy as it sounds. Seemed as if I was the host and they were the newcs. Liudvika had a kind smile on her face, but Johanna seemed a bit nervous. Which was only my fault; they were expecting me in August, and it was then October. Almost November?! My timing was a big surprise for everybody including myself. I emailed the School people just after I'd safely received the boarding pass, only once I was totally certain no other signature or stamp would be required to finally take the flight. Which all happened only the day before; last night, as a matter of fact, before the suitcase went missing. I could understand why Johanna was nervous, but there was nothing to be concerned about.

I started to explain everything. We sat down on the white couch. The black rucksack was sitting behind me, which I pulled gently toward myself.

She first asked me if I would like anything to drink; I was thirsty for water. She told me all about the School, & how things would be working there. And I told them about the missing suitcase, wondered if there were any shops in town that I could get some clothes. They suggested some places. I, myself, couldn't understand why I'd asked that question. I wouldn't really need to buy new clothes, I was not even going to bother with that; I already had about enough in my suitcase. What would I do with the new clothes, then, once the suitcase was back; there was no empty space. Was I supposed to throw them in the yellow clothing bin, so that someone would buy it from the second-hand shop?! Or, would they be recycled and reused as raw material?! Which seemed very unlikely to happen. Should I give them away? To someone who might need them, maybe to friends who already had enough clothes?! However, there are always people who are in need, people who had lost their homes. It was the case of forest fire in our region; it might be the storm or the flood elsewhere. Later, around summertime, where I needed more light shoes rather than my winter hiking boots, Luís told me about a charity in town where you could both donate, and pick clothes if you needed some. I hadn't lost anything during the fire, though I would've appreciated a pair of light summer shoes. I was told that I could return the items back before I left. We never visited the charity, though. The hiking boots weren't so bad after all; I still have them on every day to this date.

Buying new clothes was out of the frame. It was eventually going to be a piece of clothing thrown away by someone else instead of me. I'm not even sure if I listened to Johanna and Liudvika as they gave me the directions to the shop. It was best if I washed my tee shirt in the evening before I went to bed, & put it back on in the morning once it was nice and dry. The air was warm, perhaps a bit chilly and damp at night, but even a few hours of the morning sun would be the perfect drier; all good condition to wash my black top which had started to smell incredibly funny.

Later during the day, I was introduced to the friends who lived in the School; we were going to share the space. RJ told me about a huge fire that had happened a couple days before, & that the air had started to clear out only that morning. He talked about a huge brown cloud in the sky, light gray ashes falling from the sky looking like dreamy snow. It was a catastrophe, a very scary disaster indeed. But, I couldn't help but be intrigued by the stories I was being told. Sounded more like an adventure you're invited to dive in deep. I obviously had no idea what I was thinking about. I should've been more careful with what I wished for, as they say said. Well, I was not.

We woke up to the same brown cloud in a couple days. If I remember correctly, it was the afternoon after the party by the river. The fire was even more intense now, it was much closer to the School. We were surrounded by the fire from three different directions. In other words, the whole valley was burning, the houses, birds, animals, sheep in the cheese factory, insects. And humans. It is a scary thing to even imagine losing all your stuff in just a few hours, everything you keep in your home. Betty and John, a couple that we met in the village around the springtime, told us how their house was burned down; all they had left were the clothes they were wearing during the accident, & what they had in the car with them. More devastating is when you know there were many others just like them. It's impossible to comprehend what you might be going through at that moment. The only thing you should really be saving is yourself, your loved ones. John was looking for the right word for a few moments to describe peoples' reactions facing giant flames attacking from everywhere. Panicked, in the end he said, they were fully panicked. Running around, not knowing what to do. The stress had made big chaos, made it even harder to figure a way out. The roads got blocked for the tension, and the chances of surviving were down to one if it wasn't zero. It really is a scary picture to imagine.

We were absolutely panicked too, even though the deadly flames were still relatively far away from us. Fortunately, our only concern at the moment was the big brown cloud above us. We kept going through our options in case the fire surrounded us closely. We didn't have any ideas about what should be done. Some of us believed that we needed to join the rest of the people of the town at the gym. It didn't make any sense to us, RJ and I; loads of people were already there, people with problems as real as losing lives. Something far more blasting than the smoky air, & a giant brown cloud above our heads. We believed we needed to stay where we were; it would be safe in the School.

RJ had been going on long runs almost every afternoon, he'd been exploring the area on foot for as far as he could. He said that the fire was still very far away, it would take days before the trouble could reach us. All the hills around us needed to char before the School would drown in flames. Unlike RJ, my argument was not based on any solid evidence whatsoever; it was just the naïve optimist in me who couldn't stop believing that things were going to be alright; nothing bad would happen in the end. Besides, the weather forecast was predicting heavy rain in the next few days. Well, of course, I was as well considering the very special location of the School, how it was set by the corner of the valley, rather more secluded and a bit safer. I imagined where I would shelter if we ever had to leave the School. Perhaps by the river; the running water should keep us safe. RJ reminded me that suffocation is the cause of death for most of the cases. The black smoke, not the fire itself; I'd be dead by the river. The naïve optimist couldn't stop checking the weather forecast, looking forward to the rain, though it was only the golden balls of the sun for the rest of the week, the clouds kept skipping to the next day. The only cloud was the brown one, getting bigger and darker every hour, preparing us for a tragic death.

Julie was concerned the most about the whole situation, mainly because she was exposed to so many fires back in her home country. She was one of the neighbors of Kinta. When she first came to us, she simply warned us about the potential threats that we might not be aware of. She suggested that it wouldn't be such a bad idea if we stayed at Naja's for the night; it would be much safer to stick together. They had cars, David and Robert, other neighbors of Kinta. We could've hopped on, driven away, & escaped the savage fire as soon as we felt it breathing down our neck. She couldn't possibly stress more how serious the situation was, bless her soul, which we understood, but had not much of an idea what to do about.

The School, or the houses down the village didn't seem to be very different if the fire ever reached us. In fact, the School was totally sound comparing to Kinta which was only a few hundred steps away from the gas station, I think I already told you about the place.

Although, Julie was very persuasive. So, we packed our backpacks, & finally agreed to stay at Naja's for the night; Liudvika was away during the fire. The brown suitcase, which was by then delivered to me thanks to the department of lost and found, was put next to my friends' stuff inside the small safe tunnel in the basement. I tapped on the devoted luggage twice for good luck, & left the School with the black rucksack on my shoulders; it was holding anything as important as myself. I was worried. It wasn't just my belongings that I was worried about, it was the suitcase itself that I couldn't afford to lose. I had already experienced its absence not so long ago, as though it was gone for good.

Naja greeted us nicely in the house; the door was open once we arrived. She welcomed us with some drinks. Can't tell what, perhaps some tea it was, or some red wine. Including Liudvika's room in the plan, there was enough space for all of us to sleep well enough. Hoping that things would look better in the morning, we fell into a very shallow sleep. The optimist in me believed that it would soon rain, & the weather forecast was simply wrong. I couldn't stop thinking about the suitcase. I fell in and out of sleep by the noises I heard near the morning, neighbors talking, dogs barking. Expecting somebody to knock on the door any moment, where we'd have to escape without our things, drive away, & fade into the wobbly image of the heat, and the smoke, and the loud mysterious growling. I promised myself that the first thing to do would be to shred once again, keep it as light as the rucksack which I could simply grab and run off. I never really did that.

As was expected, nothing had happened that night; we returned to the School safely in the morning. We didn't unpack; it hadn't yet rained, & the sky was still brown. For some strange reason, things felt to be calmer the next morning, very calm as a matter of fact. As if the hazard was gone, & we didn't need to worry about anything. Perhaps it was the infamous stillness before the storm that they keep referring to. Because things were only getting worse.

During the day we lost the power completely, & candles became our close friends. Before we lost the network connection, we heard about Johanna's house that was partially burnt. The olive tree in her yard was now gone. Chris and Dave's shed in the corner of their garden was destroyed too; they are a couple of close friends. In fact, if their neighbor hadn't turned out the growing fire, their house would be gone as well; they weren't in the town at the time of the fire attack. I visited their house a few months after, their half-burnt yard, trees and plants, melted and deformed leftovers of the shed, their antiques and souvenirs and the collection of things. The whole valley was black, for as far as eyes could see. The valley beyond our village, the one that I somehow managed to snooze through on the bus trip I was on. Funny how I missed it simply by shutting down my eyelids for a few minutes.

We heard that loads of people had gathered in the town; they had nowhere else. They said over eighty people had died already in the past couple days. Eighty, that's a very scary number, eighty people! I don't think my family would be eighty people altogether. If I had to write down the name of my friends on a piece of paper, I wouldn't be able to reach up to eighty. Or, if I was to organize a party, I don't think I could've invited eighty guests. That's such a big number. The scariest part was when we realized this incident wasn't specific to our trip; it happened every year. More as a tradition, some type of cultural occasion or some kind. Multiple times a year, I'd better say, not just once or twice.

Losing the connection, & not having a way to communicate with the world only meant one thing: we had to keep our eyes on the hills around to spot the fire as soon it reached our view. We were ready to run away. There were some lousy bicycles in the School; there was still hope, a rather shabby way out. The police also knew about us, the residents of the School; they would protect us. We even thought of staying up until morning, wondering if there would be some wine for our spontaneous party. It would soon rain. In the morning, the sun would be up, & things would be fresh and clean again.

Well, things turned out differently. Julie and Naja came to us later in the evening. They were seriously panicked, furiously asking us to get our things, & sit in the car as fast as we could; the fire was there. It had finally reached us. We could see it burning down the hill on our left. Although, we couldn't see it from the School. Naja caugh it down the road by the small bridge over the stream on her way back to Kinta. There was no need to rush all that bad, the fire still had a long way to come. However, it was fast, and it was red, and indeed very angry; even the sound of the flames roaring with the wind from afar was too terrifying.

Julie stood on the last step of the stairs down the gate, said that we needed to hurry, there was no time. What about our bags, we thought altogether. No time for bags, she said. RJ and I looked at each other. We both heard her, perhaps laughed madly on the inside because it was actually very funny. The pain was mutual: we couldn't. If everything was going to blacken, burn down to ashes, with the seared ground and toasted soil still smoky for days to come. If there would be nothing left but a dead valley, losing our bags would've been too much to afford. They were too precious to leave behind. The bags were all we had, it wasn't the time to leave them in the basement, it wasn't the time to take a nap on the bus.

In the end, we had enough time to take a few trips back and forth to the School, to collect some more stuff, & save more items. I believe some of us even grabbed a pillow for a comfortable sleep wherever we had to crash for the night. We watched the fire by the road over the bridge, getting closer to us with every trip.

It rained in about an hour after our escape, forty-five minutes or so. Good thing I was wearing my blue raincoat, & had my black gumboots on the whole day. The rain was foreseen, I was ready; it was just not getting there.

Even though we were in the middle of a serious disaster, I somehow cannot comprehend how it all happened. Can't really rely on my memory on that; things were far more confusing than seen. Perhaps it was for the smoke which we got used to very slowly; it smelled like a tragic barbeque party. We inhaled it constantly, every second more than the one before. It reminded me of a poem that a friend of mine had read to me years ago, Rana, you might recall her from somewhere. I had to think about the words for a moment to fully remember the piece; the memory was dusty. But it was about the fishes swimming beneath, asking each other curiously, what about the water; they had not ever seen anything but.

It rained. We danced without music over the bridge for one good minute. The sad stories kept coming for days after, weeks, months. It was bitter to see this whole event was becoming rather ordinary. Every summer, by the end of spring, or the beginning of autumn.

We were soaking wet by the time we were back in the School; the rain was wild. Back with our bags and everything else we dragged around. What a blissful rain. I slide the brown suitcase under my bed, didn't really bother to unpack, soon, there was going to be another bus to catch.

Story For Five

The black rucksack was successfully squeezed under my seat. There wasn't much room for my legs, so I had to think for a moment how to sit. It was a common issue, & I was fairly used to the situation. I always manage to fit my legs somewhere. The only real problem comes from the soles of the boots; I wish they were clean so that I could put them anywhere. The bag was way too heavy for me to lift up to the overhead compartment; I don't believe that it would've fit there anyway. The overhead compartments of train wagons are technically a narrow shelf for a small briefcase and a summer jacket of exquisite passengers, who elegantly meet other travelers over tea or coffee; people who magically manage to stay light.

I sat by the window without really knowing my seat number. In certain train lines, the number of your seat doesn't seem to matter much. Anyone can sit anywhere, and it's okay. Unless the person who actually thinks this is an important issue gets on board, & it all becomes a huge disaster. One winter afternoon, I was riding on a train to visit a town for the day. An older lady started walking down the aisle, holding her ticket tightly in her hand, looking up the number of the seats till she found the one. Somebody was taking her seat, which she wanted back. All of a sudden, the numbers started to be spoken and heard, everyone moved. She made all the passengers sit at the exact point their tickets asked them to. It was complete chaos. Thankfully, it was a small train, it didn't take very long.

I've come to notice that some people don't care much about the window seat when it comes to trains either. I don't understand, how can they not?! Some people even claim they get a slight headache when they sit by the window, or their stomach feels upset, which is out of my comprehension. They say they'd rather stare down to the floor, or watch the back of the front seat. They are the kind of people who cannot really read on the train or on the bus because they would feel fuzzy.

Well, different people, different levels of sensitivity, I wouldn't know. I don't think I'd ever be able to give up a window seat. It is a big deal on the airplanes, for some obvious reason, people are rather meticulous about it. It must be for the grand view, the geometrical shapes of the farmlands beyond the windmills. It makes you feel powerful once you see it all from above, to be able to witness nature change so rapidly, pass by different territories or countries so quickly. The views are always stunning no matter what your vehicle of choice would be. It's hard to say if one is more beautiful than the other, or which angle is more mesmerizing. Watched from the airplane, or tracking the railroad through back alleys of the town along the horizon. Trains stories are told in a pastel voice. Most of the rails have been lined decades ago, you get to trip through old bridges and stations left from the past. Some stations even look abandoned, as if no departures would take place, no arrivals, no hellos or goodbyes; the clocks still work however, humans leave their own traces behind.

I glanced back at the wire shelves by the door. Took a look at the gray backpack to be sure that it was still there. It had been taking such good care of me, especially the night before at the airport. It was a very late flight, we landed even later than expected. The weather was stormy, the pilot had to wait to catch the right moment to take off; we waited for quite a bit. My plan for the night was to stay at the airport regardless, our late arrival only restricted my chances to spot the perfect corner as the perfect bed. As a matter of fact, my initial plan was to camp on the beach. It was summer, & it was down south where it's supposedly warm almost all year around. But not that year, I guess; the winter was rainy, and the spring was wintery; my plans were badly timed.

The airport was almost closed when we landed. In the corner by the baggage delivery hall, I found a set of stairs which would lead to the office loft, airline agencies, management room, lost and found and such. Seemed it was going to be uninterrupted all throughout the night, so I climbed up. There were some metal seats along the hall, but there was not much more to it. I preferred sleeping on the floor rather than being miserable on the comfortless chairs. I quite like sleeping on the floor, on a nice clean carpet. The stone floor wasn't really a good condition, but it was not taken for granted either. At least the hard surfaces could help ease the tension on my back caused by carrying all the heavy bags.

I found a plug to charge Four-Es, my new old smartphone, & camped on the dark granite stones of the narrow hallway. It wasn't overall terrible, except it was cold. Even if I spread the sleeping bag underneath, the coldness of the stone floor would leak through. So I didn't bother taking it out, not that I was too lazy or too slow. A mat would've been nice, but I didn't have mine with me. I couldn't even remember what happened to it when I was emptying my rental flat. I was very tired to think. I placed my back on my chunky gray backpack, laid my legs on the floor. My eyes were shut before I knew. The cold stone floor didn't seem to be much of a problem at first, I was too exhausted that I'd fall asleep anyhow. The bag was providing a satisfying level of comfort for my upper body. After a few moments, the airport was completely shut. Most of the lights went out, it was very quiet. The fans and the air conditioners were humming the sound of the sea, waves coming forth one by one.

I didn't feel any discomfort until after the first cycle of a nap, where the floor began to feel too cold for my legs. I tossed and turned, left and right, again and again, but I couldn't settle. I believe it was around the third nap that I decided this nightmare needed to be altered. I took a book out of the black rucksack, can't quite tell what I was reading at the moment, Hemingway, Virginia Woolf, or perhaps Bob Dylan; I placed it under the edge of my hip where it was touching the floor. I took my notebook and put it underneath my ankle to create a space between my body and the ice-cold stones. Technically, I was sleeping in the air. After each move in my sleep, intending to take the pressure off the left hip to the other, I had to adjust the books to be back in their precise places. Although, it was still fairly cold. Not even the honest black jacket of mine was helping. My bones were cold, inside of my bones. I needed a hot shower, fire, or the direct summer sun to get heated through.

The airport was generously delivering their network without a passcode; I connected my smartphone online. I wondered if I still had a chance to picnic casually on the beach in the morning. Gray clouds, wind, & the rain was predicted; the beach was out of the frame. It was an odd kind of weather. We had to put on our jackets to stop shivering from the cold; that's odd. Then the summer arrived in one day. In the evening, we took off our jumpers and trousers, went to bed under the blankets and quilts. The next morning we woke up to a sun that would melt your unprotected skin; it was already forty degrees. I believe it was the end of July, or the first day of the month of August. I had planned a lot of swimming for that summer since we had an excellent river in the town, but the opportunity didn't arise all that often. The very few hot days in May and June were our precious gems amongst all the gray days of the spring. They were not taken for granted, however, we made sure we'd take advantage of them the best. Dinner parties in our yard, accompanied by red wine, & more wine as for the pudding. Movie nights in the right-hand terrace, long walks around the valley, picking cherries and wild berries along the way. And luckily, we managed to go for a swim a couple afternoons which, as always, happened spontaneously.

It was one very lazy afternoon at Kinta, fully escorted with foreseen aftereffects of the party we had in the School the night before. The month of June was about to come to an end. It had been a while since I'd started living in Kinta, in the room upstairs with Naja and Liudvika. It was past noon when we finished the breakfast, & lounged on the terrace to rest the meal off. We wanted to believe that the summer was already there; it had been nice and warm for a few days in a row. But the weather forecast had predicted cold winds for next week, the sun would hide away soon again.

Naja was sitting on the stairs of the terrace catching some sunlight. Liudvika was sitting near her, but under the shadow; her skin wasn't pigmented enough for a bright sun of the south. Vitsi, a fifty-year-old man, one of the recent neighbors of Kinta, was sitting on the other side of our narrow terrace, or would it be considered as a balcony?! I was leaning my back against the open door. Neil was sitting by me, & Yuri was lounging on the other side. I can't quite remember where the rest of the crew were, friends who stayed over after the event. I probably didn't pay much attention to them, or care enough to see if they were enjoying the day. I guess I saw them playing in the yard with our funny bicycles. It didn't matter. Times were hard, the path was again at its sharpest turn, and the future was dark. Isn't it always the way it is?! However, there was something nice about the afternoon. It was a calm and still day, sunny and warm; the nicest weather we ever had in a very long while, or, could ever wish for. We had eaten food; not much to complain.

By that point, we'd held enough celebratory occasions so that I could clearly see the following day. There would be a dislocation between the head and the neck and the shoulders, which would cause a peculiar irritation where you wouldn't feel quite like yourself. Depending on the night and the context of the event, it could be mild, or, very advanced. Some days it was only sleep deprivation to get me to feel wobbly. Some other days, it would show up as mysterious stress and an insoluble sadness. Where I couldn't figure for what reason.

On that particular day, it was the combination of all, everything was happening at the same time. And nothing was helping me feel better. Water, coffee, black tea. Sometimes a micro nap would be a warm broth for the stomach, some fresh air as a gentle hug in the lungs. I would expose my face to the sun, to collect more of that precious light.

A slow breakfast to feast on was the next hope to feel good. We gathered around the glass table. A big bowl of salad with whatever vegetable we found in the fridge: cucumber, tomato, carrot, bell pepper or leafy greens. The salad would be varnished with apple cider vinegar and a big splash of extra virgin olive. The soft bitter smell of the dark green oil would be enough to get you back to yourself. But, I guess it was a tough day for me; the smell filled the air as I tossed the salad carelessly.

Breakfast wouldn't be breakfast without eggs. We would fry them in butter in a way that the yolks were perfectly creamy, of course, runny, and salty. If we had the right ingredients in hand, we would make it into a delicious Menemen. Though, I believe some of us turned the eggs into a tasty omelet, which, to be perfectly honest, I don't really care much for. A part of the ceremony was to get the slices of bread toasted and browned on the edges as the breakfast was coming together. It was all very easy until the electric toaster stopped working all of a sudden. We had to experiment with the oven, or our terrible frying pan. Sometimes I would put the bread directly on the hub on a low fire. Personally, the only reason I was eating the bread was to spread some butter on it, and top it with a slim sheet of the dark paste of yeast extract. It was one of our latest, and best discoveries in the traveling kitchen. Cheese and salami almost never went missing from our table. And a glass of wine, or two to keep the festivity rolling.

Not even a fabulous meal as such made me feel any better.

So I planned to do nothing for the rest of the day. It was a good idea to do nothing, it was almost necessary. We sat still on the terrace for a few moments. I remembered that I hadn't yet gone swimming, & it was going to be the first dip of the year. All of a sudden, the river trip started to sound brilliant: have a swim, get a couple of drinks, & continue doing nothing there. Good thing that people of the terrace were all on the same page; the idea was appealing to everyone.

Vitsi suggested calling his usual taxi driver so that we'd be there in about five minutes. He thought about it for a second, held the small screen of his telephone closer to his face to find his contact. He had a very light shake in the hand; the years have not been kind to him. He said we could have a nap there as he was pushing the button to find the chauffer's number, said he fancied getting wet, it was such a hot day. Nobody said nothing. It felt clumsy, I thought I'd better say something, or this was going to turn into an awkward pause. I said that a swim would be nice. The silence stretched on, which would soon wash the sourness of the words he's spread. But, it didn't stop him from speaking. He took a deep drag off the cigarette he was holding in his other hand, said he would put me in the river, as he blew the dense smoke out of his mouth. Nobody said anything. I swallowed my laugh; it was best to remain muted.

He'd put me in the river, he said. It was the kind of statement that you needed a few seconds to fully comprehend, digest, & start making jokes about. A lot of jokes turned around the terrace, we had quite a lot of good laughs. Vitsi probably didn't understand what the jokes were about, he kept smoking his cigarette, trying to find the phone number of the driver. I don't think he heard himself; too intoxicated perhaps. The jokes were mostly made by Neil and Yuri, if not all; they were funny people. Although, I can't quite remember the stream of the jokes for I was constantly laughing. I couldn't take that image out of my head; a fifty-year-old man was putting me on the surface of the running water, I would drift weightlessly like a leaf. The water would take me with it wherever it went, I really didn't need to worry much about anything. Except for the absence of the sun; what if it was gone?!

The echoes of the picture remained with me for almost all day. We crossed the river to reach the sands dusted annually on the upper banks by the edge of the town; I lied on the sands. It was the second round that the municipality had to sprinkle the pale yellow sands to make it a comforting beach; the first sand was washed off by the storm. It was quite unusual to have such heavy storms around those months of the year; the summer would usually be early there. It must've been an exceptional year in any sense, though we didn't know about the future which was only getting worse. Dreadful as it was for the rest of the globe, just as it is now every year. Everything seemed to be a bit upside down. We were looking forward to the summer, but the storm would strike every few days. We would only get more restless. The river was still muddy from the last violent rain. It was suggested not to drink the tap water, or at least filter it before consumption. Although, I would skip it mostly, & would drink it regardless. Things weren't perfect, not really a good condition, one glass of water more or less.

We had everything to enjoy an afternoon by the river. We were doing nothing. I took a swim in the muddy water, I'd missed swimming madly. I believe it was the only thing that could help me feel better. The water washed away my waste; felt nice for a change. It didn't really wash anything anywhere, it was only a mind game. A decent excuse to forget about reality. To feel good, think about happiness, whether it was truly over-rated, to consider the beautiful things I used to see in the corners I looked, muddy or not; the beauty was still very present, I had only forgotten which angle was the right way to see. Days were coming and going, occupied by all the responsibilities to remain human, things that needed to be sorted on a daily basis, one day to the next, & the one after that.

The sun was touching my face and my body. It was so nice that I didn't even bother putting on sunscreen. The sun was on and off behind the clouds, the breeze would keep a good balance on the temperature. After a few minutes of constant shadow, I had to open my eyes to realize that the sun had finally sunk behind the trees of the hill in front of us; the breeze was going to be chilly from then on. I asked Neil and Yuri if they were ready to head back, and if they'd like to walk. They said that it was actually a good idea.

The airport had become loud enough to let me know that it was time to leave; it was morning. There was one thing left to do before leaving. I had to declare my arrival to the border police. I walked to the information desk, asked who I should meet for that case. The lady behind the counter suggested using the phone in the corner; I could ask whatever question I had in mind from the person on the other end of the line. Turned out there was no way I could declare or register my arrival from the airport. I was given a couple names and addresses to attend; it was going to be a headache.

I couldn't see a point in going to the beach if it was going to be cloudy and cold. It seemed sad to picnic on a potentially rainy day. Besides, most of my morning was going to be occupied by the paperwork. The plan had to be canceled.

I was trying to figure out the right timing, which trains to get on in order to catch the last bus to the village. Platform number nine, I believe, or number four, was it?! I took a walk around downtown before I got myself to the train station, passed by the alleys, had a look on a few churches from the outside; I had seen so many churches by that point that adding more to the collection didn't sound that very exciting anymore. My bags were heavy, I've already had a long morning, so I couldn't go through the trouble.

I looked through a few cafés and pastries. The menus didn't seem to be so interesting, even though I hadn't eaten anything yet. I couldn't remember the last time I actually ate, but I certainly wasn't planning on having flour, sugar and fat for lunch, or breakfast, or whatever the meal was called. I needed some kind of warm salad, some soup, perhaps a couple of well seasoned creamy yolks. I could've gone to the supermarket to put together a decent meal for myself, but the bags were too heavy. It was best to skip another meal. I'd already figured that you wouldn't die without food for a few days. Death is near, but it doesn't come easy.

As I was walking around the town, I couldn't help but notice how similar it was to the other towns I'd visited or lived before. The general structure of the town, the uphill and downhill, the stairs to climb up these hills, the breath-taking views awaiting you on the final step. There was a wide body of water running through the city which divided it into two, & the two pieces were connected back by a bridge. Sounds quite familiar. I was missing my territory, places that I perfectly knew all about. The discomfort of unfamiliarity was sometimes so bold and so loud that I unconsciously looked for relatable cultural and habitual patterns. The way people commute, socialize, dine, party. The selective perception might be a bit more forceful when you miss your tribe. I wasn't falling for the cafés which looked exactly like one another, same lightings and decorations, similar chairs, stools, or tables. Or the flashy graffiti of the back alleys. The delightful face of the town remains out of sight. The tea houses back in the City that many tourists would easily overlook, the very small wooden stools; what was I missing there?! I guess the key to witnessing the difference would be to reach paths walked less. If the luck is on my side, I'd meet local friends who know a cool place to shoot coffee. They get to lunch where they trust the chef, dance in rooms with windows to watch the sunrise on the outskirts of town as the party takes a bend.

I looked through a café as I passed it by, noticed a man drawing the glorious church in front. He took the smallest sip of his coffee. I needed some coffee. Shooting a few strong shots was one of my newest habits that kept developing for as long as I lived in the country. I would often sprinkle cinnamon on top of the crema to make it a small pudding. Every place brings its own habits. Most of which fade out as soon as I'm gone. I smelled the coffee, and craved; it was nice to be back. The man put down the white cup, & I walked on; I couldn't hesitate a second to stop.

I was following the map to get to the train station. Thankfully, it was all downhill, I didn't have to climb with the big load on my person. I read the names of the streets and the alleys which matched my offline map; I was on the correct path. I arrived at the pinned point where the train station was located. But, there was no evidence of any stations whatsoever. It was a small parking lot for city buses. It was where the drivers could get some rest, drink some coffee or tea, take a break in between their shifts, and let the engine cool down. It didn't seem right. I checked the map again. It was a bit intimidating to go ahead and ask the drivers, but I had to, it was late. I was not looking forward to missing the last bus back to the village.

It's funny how I, yet again, managed to be late. Isn't that funny?! I had to take care of some paperwork which was inevitable, though, morning is a long time, what was I doing then?! It requires a serious amount of experienced skills to be able to accomplish such a thing, to be late for almost every occasion. I walked across the street to reach one of the drivers standing by his bus. I greeted the group, raised my head hello to the ones standing further away. I said I was looking for the train station. They looked at each other wondering what I was talking about. If they understood me correctly, there were no train stations there. The driver standing near me said it was the wrong address, I must go elsewhere. So far, so obvious. He asked me to walk along so that he could show me the address. I did; things get clumsy when two people don't speak the same language. He pointed to the end of the alley in front of us, said that the station was there, on the left; he pointed left with his arm. Just to be sure, I asked if I needed to go left, even though we didn't speak the same language. He told me not to worry, I was going to see it already once I reached the end of the alley. The alley didn't seem to be very long. I thanked them, said a loud goodbye as I hurriedly left.

I reached the train station. The building looked magnificent. I was glad that I chose the train instead of the bus only because I was curious to see the station; a good call. Looking at the building was in a way watching the past; not much had changed since the station was established. I have been to even older places, but that's the charm to the trains that makes me wonder so. More as a tunnel to travel through time, take the train and watch the view that people of the past would watch. The landscape doesn't change all that fast as long as it's not interrupted by humans. I climbed up the stairs as I looked at the huge clock on top of the tall doorways; it was the last few minutes. There was a group of tourists gathered in the corner, listening closely to what their tour guide had to say about the station. I wish I could understand, even if I could catch a sentence. I had to run; I hadn't bought my ticket yet. I found my way to the ticket booths by the end of the hallway to the left. I was shocked to see what was ahead of me: a long line of people waiting. And there was no other way but to wait with them.

Well, eventually, as you might be able to tell, I made it to the train one way or another. I put my elbow on the side of the window, & made myself comfortable. There wasn't much water left in the blue bottle, I took a small sip. I was sweating underneath my clothes. My bones were not cold anymore. I thought of my next ride, the path that I had to walk from the train station to the coach station to catch our old bus. I was predicting which driver would have the shift; they were two. I had taken the bus for a few times already that I was rather familiar with the schedule. Then I wondered how many trips I'd taken with that bus so far; it was the fifth ride, I guess. The number wasn't all that charming when I counted. I counted again. I could make up a story for five in my head to make it sound lucky, a good fortune for my return to the School, even though the stay wasn't going to be so long. I could see myself taking the bus back, to return, or I'd better say, go elsewhere. As they always say, the path of going and returning is not the same. Thankfully, I wouldn't know what the future would hold. Not to know a thing about the future is the bliss we yearn for. Daydreaming would be pointless if I knew that the summer was going to be cold. No pleasure in imagining a perfectly hot afternoon, walking about the countryside in shorts, taking naps on the grass with a decent layer of sunscreen on the skin after a casual lunch picnic. A summer with jackets & raincoats, frozen toes with the trusty scarf around the neck, and a cup of ginger tea on the side to keep warm would only leave us broken-hearted.

Six Different People

    Extremely careful not to trip over my own footsteps, I started walking down the stairs. It was hard to watch the next step with the black rucksack hanging in front of my chest; the gray one was occupying the back. They were both fairly heavy, not too dramatic to make the walk impossible, but certainly a great pain on my person to get me to reevaluate my belongings and things that I stuffed in. Somehow, in some ways, it was torture more than anything else.

And I was tired, it had been quite a long journey. I had taken the bus which took me thirty-something hours to finally be where I was: walking down the metro station. It was an incredible trip in any sense, but, I can't ignore the aftereffects, a life-time of exhaustion for constantly being seated on the bus for more than a day. I was also bearing a mild depression for the recent departure, all the hugs and goodbyes after a very long party. A life had ended for all, things soon would be forgotten. Fully aware of the happy ending awaiting by the end of the subway ride, I embraced the pain. Soon, I would take some rest, sleep on a bed with white sheets. I would be there in less than half an hour.

For this trip, I'd decided to take the bus for no solid reason. The financial difficulties, however, was a major consideration, as well as the therapeutical aspect of it. The air pollution, also. Flying is not all healthy for the globe, which is not really an issue these days. It's been a few months that most of the flights are canceled all over, except for a few trusted airlines; the future of the airways seems to have been permanently modified.

Long story short, I'm glad I did take the bus. It was everything I ever wished for a trip, the privilege of taking my time to get to point number two.

As I was booking the ticket online, I imagined myself sitting on the bus riding on the road. It's nice to be on the road every so often. Where you don't have many responsibilities for the present moment, no easy connection to take care of things back home, or do the work, or anything else you would do on an ordinary day; you just need to be. Road-trip should be a grand hobby, I've always been a huge fan. To do nothing but to watch the landscape change slowly before your eyes, getting closer to the last stop every minute.

It wasn't the longest bus trip I'd been on. I have another trip on the resume which took me over forty hours, counting in the hours wasted at the border of the two neighboring countries.

Not sure if I could ever top that record, if I ever should. You never know, the future might make it happen.

Regardless of the sitting, it was a nice trip. I was a bit confused towards the end, lost in time and space. I had to transfer into another bus after the hour twenty-six or so, in one of the capitals on the route. I got off the first bus, thanked the funny driver, and walked about the station to find my second bus. The next departure was in a couple of hours, so I took my time. I had to go up and down the stairs a few times, ask different agents for different directions, show my traveling documents to different officers once they asked for my passport; I finally found my bus. There was no seat number on the ticket, nothing that I could find. So, I sat by the window in the first row. I hugged the black rucksack to catch my breath for a moment before I had to fit it under my seat.

As soon as I thought things were all okay, and I could relax till I reached the final destination, the driver aired the surprising news. He said that it wasn't really passing by the town that I'd purchased the ticket for. I was either misinformed, or something went wrong in the system. He suggested taking the train from the town very near where I was going. He also said that the train trips were quite frequent and very speedy. Things were okay, everything got sorted. It was only one extra step.

I eventually arrived in the town by sea, where it's famous for its winds. I had to figure out the public transport to get myself to the precise door. I wasn't so sure where I was, or which direction I needed to be heading. I'd pinned the location on my map, but where was it really?! There were all kinds of questions floating before my eyes as I was leaving the central train station. Which street should I be heading toward, what was the number of the bus? Where is the north?! Should I be taking the tram, which stops to get off? I wished from the bottom of my heart that the bags were slightly less heavy so that I could walk there, just as simple as that. It was less than forty minutes on foot, my offline map said, which was a shorter walk than from the School to the supermarket.

It was raining. I had to ask other people how to get myself there. Perhaps I asked six different people, & I was given six different directions. I ended up walking up and down the avenue a few rounds since everyone had their own route, & would recommend a different opinion; I just wished someone would tell me the right one. And people were all very kind, it was nice to see I was welcomed. Some would even be slightly concerned as they saw the heavy loads on me, as if I was their distant friend. Wet from the rain, tired as a racing horse; they would've been nicer if they knew I was hungry too. I hadn't seen any mirrors since, but I'm sure I looked pale, & I had dark circles around my eyes. I should've treated myself with a decent meal, something hot in a bowl to hold and heat my fingertips, to smell the taste, & regain the power that had somehow vanished throughout the trip for no tangible reason.

It was the subway at last. I was looking for the ticket booths, but, I found none. There aren't so many ticket booths left in this day and age. There's a machine for everything, or an online application for the smartphone. Each system works differently: sometimes you have to scan the screen of your phone on a machine, sometimes they track you down automatically. In a way, they punch your digital ticket for you so that you wouldn't have to be bothered with such a simple task. Ticket booths would work fine for me. I meet a person, greet them, ask a question or two to make sure that things were okay; it's good to know that things are alright.

I used to enjoy subway rides when I was younger, can't tell what it really was that I loved so much about them. I would take the subway whenever I could. It felt efficient and sustainable, as if I was doing something good for society, and for the environment. What I found to be quite peculiar was that you'd go down under the ground somewhere, take the vehicle that supposedly was moving forward, but you don't really get a sense of going anywhere since it's all black out the window.

Eventually, you would climb up the stairs to a neighborhood on the other side of the town. This used to fascinate me. People looked interesting as well. There was boredom, some kind of exhaustion on their faces, as if they were sad about something; perhaps it's because there's nothing to see out the window. All we have to do would be to wait to arrive at the destination, at least we're getting somewhere.

I didn't notice any gates where you would pass to get to the platform. I walked on. I needed to ask a local how the subway system worked. But there wasn't anyone around, empty hallways all over. I reached a point where the path would divide in two directions, left or right, the train to go, or to return. I tried to remember what I was told. The guy who helped me with the address mentioned the name of my stop, however, the names were so foreign and new that recalling them was out of my capabilities. Besides, names don't stick to my mind all that well, maybe I've talked about this before. I couldn't really tell where I was going. I already knew that I would be confused and lost, I could see it coming. I let my guts take me, hoping I'd find a person I could ask questions.

I turned left, saw a map on the wall before I took the moving stairway down to the platform. I checked the map closely, read the names of the stations, & tried to figure out which one was mine. They didn't sound familiar, none of them. I read them out loud, perhaps they'd make more sense; they didn't. I decided it was the correct line, so I walked on. Down the stairs, many other people were waiting on the platform: that's where everybody else was.

I approached the nearest people, cleared my throat to say hello. I showed them my map, the pinned location where I needed to be. I asked them if they knew where it was. They seemed to be a couple, but they were not. I imagined they might be close friends. They said they were colleagues working for the same company; they were friends. They were immigrants who had moved very recently. They were both from the same country. I didn't get to ask them if they knew each other from before, or if they'd move together. The part that I didn't quite understand was whether they lived in the same flat, or if they were only neighbors.

They told me how come they've moved. About the bad economy back in their country, constant inflation, the rate of unemployment, how it caused depression. We were speaking in a foreign language, sometimes the words wouldn't be enough to express the thoughts, but I could understand what they were saying, I could exactly understand what they were saying. The pain was live, even though we were elsewhere, far away from our lands. If we had more time, I would've asked about their town and what the local dish was. Just out of curiosity. I had already met new friends from their country back when I was living in the south, each friend from another region.

The guy was answering very kindly, he had a smile on his face which was rather reassuring. He spoke about his experiences in the new environment he was living in; they had moved recently. He promised me that I would have a great time during my stay. I believed him when he said that I would enjoy the town dearly. Meanwhile, the lady was checking the map on her phone. She said their flat was a couple blocks away from my destination, so she knew where I was going. She only needed to double-check. She was following our conversation as well, & contributing just as much. She must've had some special talent to be able to do all those at the same time.

The train arrived at the platform, & we got on board. We stood in a corner. My new friends had told me that I could purchase my ticket from a small machine inside the wagon. I put the black rucksack down by them, walked to the machine attached to the yellow pole which had a wide screen. The gray bag remained on my shoulders. It was too heavy that I didn't bother touching it. It called for superpowers to put it down, lift it off the floor, & place it on my person again; the kind of energy that I really didn't have. I glanced back at the rucksack through the crowd on my way to the ticket machine. I felt rather guilty for leaving it on the floor on its own. The floor might've been damp and wet, cold; it was most certainly dirty. But, it was with friends that I'd met only a couple minutes before, it was safe to look away.

I reached the closest machine, tapped on the screen a few times to activate it. Nothing happened. I touched the screen on different spots, maybe it was smarter than I imagined. Yet, nothing happened. I went back to the only people I knew on the wagon, there must've been a trick to the game that I didn't know of. The guy said that they don't work every now and again. Perhaps we could look the other way for once, pretend we didn't really see if anything happened or not.

Even Seven

I found myself walking up and down the station in between the columns and the benches by the railways. Pacing aimlessly would let me clarify my mind. There was some kind of vending machine in a corner that tickled my curiosity to pace toward, & have a closer look. There was no glass to see inside the machine, however, as I got closer, I noticed small white buttons on top with different cigarette logos next to them. Nothing edible. I wasn't hungry, not that I'd be able to eat anything that early in the morning.

More than anything else, I needed a telephone to make a phone call. I had my smartphone with me, but it was somewhat dead. A payphone could've been a great help, if only I could use it in a way. I had some coins in my pocket, but it wasn't the era where you could make a call with metal coins. Hopefully, those payphones still exist somewhere; someone must've saved one as an antique object.

I remember using the phones at the newspaper kiosks until very recently. The earlier version of the kiosk-phones had a slider for the coin on the side with a tall metal button on top, which would let you push down the coin as soon as the other person picked up the phone on the other end of the line. Sometimes I would forget to press the coin down, so the friend that I'd called couldn't hear me. They'd keep saying hello, hello. And I would do the same, until, in a second, I would realize that I haven't yet paid for the call. Usually, the friend would give up just as soon as I remembered to press the button. Perfect timing: they would hang up, & my coin would go to waste. Obviously, I'd have to make another call. Hopefully, I'd have another coin.

The next generation of kiosk-phones had improved significantly. The duration of the call was shown on a digital screen, so in the end, the cost of the call would be calculated based on every spoken second. It was a very efficient design. I was recently told they'd started removing them from the system as well, you might not easily find them anymore.

Walking up and down the train station, I couldn't spot any payphones. Even if there were any, I needed a telephone card in order to make the call. There weren't any shops around to buy the card, neither would they be open at that hour. I was a bit confused about the local time, couldn't tell what time it was, but it was certainly very early, probably not even seven.

It was a secluded neighborhood, didn't seem like I would find a phone anywhere near. My personal smartphone, Four-Es, had gone dysfunctional at that point for some spooky reason. A few days before, the phone ran out of battery inside the rucksack. The screen was off when I reached for it, & it didn't turn back on again. I tried charging it, plugged it in in every socket in the house, pressed the top button as hard as I could, but it wouldn't come back.

I thought it was dead, but turned out it was only taking a break. It must've been tired of constant work. A few days later, I decided to give it one last shot before I could officially call it trash. I plugged in the charger in another town. The screen glowed in my face; it was back to life. As if nothing had ever happened. Long story short, Four-Es was in a coma, so I had lost the chance of looking for free connection in the air to go online. I don't think free signals were offered in such a secluded neighborhood, but at least it was good to know that I had options.

It was the second phone I was losing in the past few months. I'm not so sure if I've mentioned that before. First, Es-Three went missing, & now it was Four-Es's turn to bail on me. It's still hard for me to admit that I lost Es-Three. Still. It was such a tragedy. It took me a few days to get over the shock, come in peace with the fact that it was gone forever, that it was actually happening to me out of all people. I would've gone searching for it if I'd noticed earlier. My eyes were still looking for it for days after. I could see its shadow amongst my stuff on the table, where I'd usually put it, or on the top corner of my bed. Sometimes I felt its weight in my pocket, other times I heard it ring. It left me so suddenly. It was completely unexpected; it took me a while to get used to it.

Es-Three being lost, & having Four-Es in a coma, I accepted that I was phoneless. It wasn't simple. Being disconnected becomes a problem after a certain point, using your credit card for online purchases, for instance, you might get lost without the offline map. Would miss the chance of recording the moment with a light touch on the screen with your fingertip. The second of a picture, holding still for a video, or listening closely to the sound that's being recorded.

A payphone would've fit the platform just perfectly. It was an early cold morning on a fairly isolated train station. There were only a couple of people waiting by the railway to catch their rides to work, or whatever business they minded. The bus stop on the front side was empty. And there would be another passenger in the corner, dialing random numbers on a rustic phone booth.

It would feel nice to drop coins into the phone one by one, hear them cling together on the inside. Looking forward to the sound of the coins dropping, I would draw imaginary circles, or push the chunky buttons more recently in the past. It would be comforting to sense the sturdiness of the grip standing by the ear welcoming the words of the conversations. As a friendly plastic hand. I do in fact use payphones quite a lot; visiting a phone booth is a simple act of making things feel secured.

I walked down the station, got closer to the very few people waiting for the train. It occurred to me that I could borrow their phones; they all had one in their pockets. But, for some vague reason, I stopped myself from reaching them, speaking with them, & asking them for a small favor. I'm sure they would happily lend me their phone, I just didn't bother.

I would not have died if I hadn't made the call, it wasn't that big of a deal. Nothing extraordinary had happened so far, nothing concerning, or dangerous; only, I had arrived earlier than expected, way earlier; I could've made the phone call later. I had to wait; nothing else to do, but to wait. I went to my bags, the gray backpack which was holding the rucksack inside, & the funky red bag that I recently bought from a so-called vintage shop. I sat between the two of them, and wedged my fingers under my armpit. A typical cold morning of autumn.

The three of us were like a sandwich; I was the component in between the two slices of bread. Even though the red bag was relatively small, yet it was nicely covering my side. Could've been an open-faced sandwich with a piece of small toast for garnish. I leaned my head against the gray bag. I was tired, the bag was keeping me from falling. My eyelids were heavy, quite a struggle to keep them open. And I couldn't see a reason why I should. It took me one second to fall asleep.

Minute Eight

 I was again sandwiched in between the two bags: the funky red one, & the tall blue backpack which was holding the black rucksack within. I'd recently purchased the blue one from a supermarket. Buying a new bag wasn't planned at all, wasn't needed, however, the discount percentage was so generous that intrigued me to pick it up, & pass it through the cash register with me. It was quite affordable, seemed like a good deal. It was equivalent to a proper meal at a restaurant. Considering that I don't really eat out very often, I could say it was as inexpensive as a couple of nutrient meals at home; I only had to sacrifice a few costly ingredients for a week, or skip food in total for a day or two in order to have the bag without affecting my very limited budget. Thinking of which, I wondered why I bought it in the first place; I really didn't need it. The gray bag was handling my things properly one way or another. Perhaps it was the bright blue color that planted the idea in my head.

The bag itself seemed to be big enough to hold all the essentials even for longer trips. It was hard to tell at the supermarket when it was empty, but it promised to be comfortable for my back as well. Although, not even the best backpack in the universe could be comfortable when it's filled with about twenty kilograms of things.

The blue bag was sitting on my left as I was gently leaning against it. The funky red was on my other side by the window as it was gently leaning against me. That made me the filling of the sandwich, a hearty concoction of fear and anxiety, glazed with exhaustion for lack of sleep, & topped with crispy stress whether or not I could make it to the airport. I didn't bother fastening the seatbelt. Who needs a seatbelt on the backseat of the car? Being squeezed in between the bags would keep you fully protected from any horrible accidents. In some countries it's against the law not to fasten the seatbelt on the backseat, some other countries don't really care. Some laws can be adjusted to your liking. You choose if you'd obey them or not; either way, you'd have to face the consequences. You have to pay the bill if you were fined by the lawmen, or you must bear the risk of injury, or even death in case of a major car accident.

I couldn't care much about the laws at that moment, or death for that matter. I only appreciated that the highway was lawless in a way; you were free to drive at your desired speed. Some believe that speed is the first ingredient for human development. Whatever you do, they say, do it fast. Even if you're making a big mistake. You'd still have time to up your game. You could experience more, therefore, live more. Sounds like a sensible theory. However, I'm not so sure if I can completely live up to that. Some days are simply slow. I wake up slowly, take a shower and dress up slowly, make coffee slowly, walk slowly. I recall the days where I would stand in the corner of the left-hand terrace, & would breathe slowly. Every inhale counted, every exhale was important. It would take a while to process the surroundings every so often, to make up the mind, to finally come up with a decision. Critical decisions usually would need more considerations. Ironically, simultaneously, they're usually the cases you must be your fastest. Forest fire, for instance, flames approaching quickly from the hill, & you have to decide whether to take the bag with you, or if there's anything you could leave behind. You might be holding an electronic airplane ticket in your pocket, & you must choose whether to fly off, or to stay. There must be another path to the future. And you'd better think fast, because there is going to be a future.

Even though we were driving relatively fast, way faster than usual, I noticed other cars would leave us in the dust. I looked at the vehicles around us, wondering what it was like on the inside. I looked through their windows. Some were families with their children sitting on the backseat; they certainly had their seatbelts fastened. The drivers' jackets and the collar of their shirts pictured an employees' life, people coming back from work. It was those hours of the day where the work would finish: leave the job, head back home. I was already warned by the dense traffic not so far away down the highway.

I ate more of the salad sitting in a container on my lap, shoved another fork full of colorful vegetables into my mouth which had been taken out of the fridge a few minutes before. I must say, it was a very tasty salad. My severe hunger wasn't the only ingredient for its deliciousness. The key to its heavenly taste, just as any other salad, must've been concealed in the dressing. It was a perfect ratio of yogurt and mayonnaise, & the prefect few drops of freshly squeezed lemon juice. I wondered what the vinegar was, red wine?! The salad was the best idea for the trip to the airport, perhaps too good of an idea. It was a huge salad, so huge that it could satiate a family of three for lunch. The size of my meal had gone out of control which was merely caused by a stressed stomach, & a pair of hungry eyes. It was such a tense afternoon. I was quite anxious since the very beginning of the day, & the day before, even the day before that.

I had already decided to miss my flight a few days after I purchased my ticket. I tried returning it, but, for some senseless reason, it would cost me more to cancel the flight; my pocket would burn either way. I had thought about it for days. It was slow thinking since it was such a crucial decision. The future would turn upside-down. Under those wild circumstances, that was the best I could come up with; staying longer seemed to be the right thing to do. Not so sure for how long, I don't think it would've been up to me anymore after a certain point.

All of a sudden, though, earlier in the afternoon, I changed my mind. I was determined to leave, take the plane, & fly away. The future became a whimsical adventure that would leave me empty-handed. I had lived another life in my head, had gone through all kinds of concerns. I'd been delighted & depressed. Nothing had happened in reality, but the world of imagination was million years ahead. I thought I was switching paths. The plan was to skip my flight to the east, take another direction, perhaps go west. I'd pictured a whole other future, a brighter one, which seemed to be worth sacrificing a lot for.

It was only earlier in the afternoon where I realized this fantastic future was limping. I started counting my personal possessions. Not a lot, yet, I couldn't afford to lose the most primary element: my very slim slice of freedom. A fork full of bright green lettuce drenched in the white dressing went into my mouth, followed by a slice of black olive; I chewed mindlessly. I thought that the dressing could've used a bit more salt, but in actuality, I was very pleased with the way it was. My daily food intake consisted of an insane amount of salt, a major heart attack was around the corner.

I finished the salad. The last bite was, of course, the egg yolks that were fully soaked in the sauce. Even though the yolks weren't creamy, & they were thoroughly cooked, I'd saved them for last. On an ordinary day, I would've coated them in a layer of salt, possibly coarse flaky sea salt. But, it wasn't really an ordinary day. The salt was out of my reach. Not very far away, though, somewhere in the lid pocket of the funky red, and some more in the blue one. I do believe I had some more in the front pocket of the black rucksack as well. The yolk crumbled in my mouth, though it was creamy in my head. There's a perfect timing to cook the eggs in the stage of soft-boiled eggs, where the whites are softly cooked, & the yolks remain molten. The recipe asks to put the eggs in boiling water, & keep cooking them for six minutes and thirty seconds. You can adjust the creaminess of the yolks to your desired consistency, considering that they become almost firm after the minute eight. Two of those yolks on your plate for the first meal of the day might be the key to happiness. However, it wasn't the time or the place to fancy perfect eggs. I drank up the rest of the dressing. Put the fork in the container, locked the lid, & carelessly put it aside.

I gave my mouth a wipe with the back of my hand as I leaned my head against the blue bag. It still smelled very new. It was its first trip out of the company packaging. It was full, stiff, packed to its maximum capacity. My things were sorted inside the bag in less than half an hour; I still can't believe how I managed to do all that so fast.

I looked out the window, watched the landscape surrounding the highway. The land was almost flat which would allow you to see things so far away: factory chimneys, buildings of corporate companies, houses, trees, birds flying in the distance. I remember I said something nice about what I was seeing, can't recall the words. I said it with a calm voice and a smile, an inner smile so that the cheer would reflect upon my voice, so that nobody would worry about anything. Wish I could remember what I said, maybe it was something about the birds. It worked out nicely. Others replied with a nice comment, & we had a graceful moment. Everything was fine. I was still breathing. My stomach was full of healthy food, perhaps a bit too full, but I wasn't hungry. I was only upset about the dream that had come alive in my imagined world. It had vanished away before I could reach it. Nothing was lost. In fact, quite the opposite, something was gained: a blue bag slightly bigger than the gray one; it could hold even more.

The Ninth Wave

The funky red bag was bloated, rather chunky; it was almost completely full. I straightened my back, & turned my weight on the hip slightly to the left to take the pressure off the right knee. I had somehow managed to hurt my person. Can't really tell how it happened, don't remember any accidents in particular to cause the injury. It must've been for all the very long walks I was taking in the name of exclusive explorations. Running was also a big part of the routine. Some days I would just wake up from a distasteful dream, & running would be the only way to drain it off the system.

The knee was taking lots of pressure, it was hurt. It must've notified me in some ways before it completely failed, I was certainly too distracted to notice. At some point, I came across a tall mirror in a clothing store where I stood still for a moment to take a good look at my person, before even considering if the color of the fabric would complement my skin color, even though I was not going to purchase the outfit to begin with. I hadn't felt so foreign in so long. The outlines were screaming a significant change in weight. I had become fat. Which all somehow backed my theory regarding the knee injury. Hours of walks, with a significant amount of water and meat and fat on the legs, might've been the worst enemy for the knee. Then I took a longer look at the funky bag behind me. There was more to the weight, it was full of my stuff.

The pain started mild, a slight irritation on the inner side of the knee cap. It must've gotten worse with every step, very quietly and slowly, without really giving me a hint. It woke me up one morning to severe pain. It was vividly there. I know I should've, but I didn't visit any doctors at that point; I didn't really put the bag down either. It was very obvious that I needed proper rest in order to heal, & feel myself again. I wasn't supposed to walk on that knee anymore, yet, I did. A lot. On a day to day basis. Consequently, the pain grew after that point. Not so slowly anymore; it found its way to the thigh, spread down to my shin, & reached down to the right foot. No wonder why it went absolutely dysfunctional in the end, & left us sealed to the ground. I don't think I considered my knee as much as I was humanly supposed to. Times were hard, days would go by in an invisible hassle, in minutes holding obscure distress in their core. Walking eased things, helped diminish the silent misery. Who'd think about the knee?! I guess it had to pay in the end.

The pain was unbearable, even standing was impossible. Every step was torture. I was limping. I would put ointment on it a few times a day, & would wrap it tightly with an elastic bandage. I would do exercises regularly, simple moves to recover the muscles. However, it only got worse, in a way that I didn't walk unless it was one hundred percent necessary for maintaining my being. Walking to the kitchen, for instance, going through the path between the bathroom and the living room a few times a day, & maybe stepping down to the yard to get some fresh air in case the boredom would get too drastic.

It was rather ignorant of me to neglect the physical aspect of my body, I must admit, a bit disrespectful, but the health of the knee was the last thing that occurred to me under those circumstances. Instead of being more responsible, I walked. Long, for hours and hours, which would be equivalent to thirteen kilometers if not more on particular days according to my dearly departed step-counter.

I was digging the world, in and out. I would walk through alleys, watch the fountain squares, monuments, sculptures, and impressive buildings all over the town. I couldn't stop picturing all the significant people of the time that had walked the same paths, only, in the past. I would wander about nature if I found myself in a village somewhere. Walking would open the windows of my mind without making much of an effort, except for taking a step forward, followed by another step, and another one after that.

These expeditions were usually celebrated with a small picnic in a park, a calm corner surrounded in nature. Not necessarily to eat, perhaps to catch a break, sip some water, breathe in deep. I would absorb what was offered, whether it was to watch crooked bodies of the trees, or take note of the shapes of the lakes, cross the rivers over the human-made bridges to see the scenery from the land on the other side. What intimidated me the most was to get lost, yet, I was intrigued to do so on purpose, to let go of the drawn lines, & go wherever the curiosity would drive. I was constantly getting lost, perhaps I told you the story of the hand-drawn maps.

The key to finding the way back was to be fully aware of the surroundings. I wouldn't drop stones behind me, or bread crumbs, but significant signs would mark the path. In forests, however, it's frightening for me to go off-trail. I had to be careful with every step, constantly keeping aware, & reminding myself of the directions. Trees are not the best indicators to distinguish the path.

Losing my way was a whole other matter in towns and cities, I was rather looking forward to it. I've spent almost all my life in such environments; I'm familiar with the scenery, the obstacles, the potential threats. Besides, you could always ask someone for directions. One early morning, I managed to rescue myself after getting lost during a slow run. It was a run to discover the upper side of the town, to visit a well-known palace nearby. It was a nice tour. Though, I got lost on the return. I kept running around for almost an hour, trying each and every direction. I was crossing in between the alleys and the main streets that I'd never been to before, looking for a familiar sign to take me back. Sometimes I would end up in the same place, which meant that I'd taken the wrong turn. I read the map at a bus stop, but it only confused me more. Finally, I met an immigrant waiting for her bus. She seemed to be going to work. She fully, yet briefly explained the structure of the neighborhood to me. Turned out I wasn't that far away, I was just running around in circles.

Thinking of which, I was eating a lot too, let's be fair, it was the only thing I would do other than walking. Food had gradually become my wheel to explore through the new culture. The grocery store was best to find the materials, & discover beyond the surface. Whatever I ate tasted great, it was barely the case of disliking something. And there were so many more to try. My palette had widened extensively since I was curious about the new tastes. I've had the most interesting food, whether it was the ingredient itself, the way it was cooked, or if it was paired with other spices and ingredients that I wasn't familiar with.

The more I ate, the more I learned. Unfortunately, the appetite started to go out of control, so, consequently, the weight went over the top.

Yet, I was hungrier than ever. None of the food I had reminded me of our lunches and dinners. The candies wouldn't take me back in time. I'd found the food to be the easiest solution to reduce stress; it was not the case of hunger. Yet, I was never satiated. It's such a curious feeling to be hungry as soon as you're done with your meal. I had to consult with a professional to find out how. The numbers on the scale concerned me greatly.

Diet seemed to be the only way to find the old me, eat what I used to eat, to put back together the pieces that I'd lost at some point. Things had become far more confusing in my head, in a way that I lost track of the very basic elements of eating, which hour would be proper for dinner, when's breakfast and such. That I couldn't decide how many squares of dark bitter chocolate to have with my coffee in the afternoon. Or as my pudding after supper. Have a bite, two, or three. I was convinced that there's something in it to make me happy; eat more, it's somewhere there. Sometimes the whole pack of chocolate would be gone; how many bites would that be, eleven?! The injured knee was only a lesson that had to be learned the hard way. I had to see some doctor for that. Although, the prescription was very obvious. All I needed was to dance, get more vitamin D. It was the sunlight that was missing from the menu to stop fearing the future, to overcome the insecurity when you don't know what's going to happen next. Or, rather, you know exactly what you'll have to go through. Same old, if not even worse.

I put the passport in my pocket. The queue was long, and fairly slow. I started emptying my pockets off the trash now that I had nothing better to do; my pockets were stuffed. Folded tissues, old receipts, scraps of paper holding an unimportant note. I found the train ticket that I took earlier in the morning. It was my return ticket back to the town. I was still thinking that the airport is out of the plan then, & I believed that the path was leading me elsewhere. The future looked very different in the morning before I took that train.

I was distracted the whole ride through, can't even tell what I was thinking of. I was so distracted that I got off the train one station before my stop, & so I had to run to make it to my appointment; I had a meeting with a consultant to clear a few facts about the future. I ran for more than one kilometer. With the funky red on the back, & the right knee that had almost completely gone off. It wouldn't be too dramatic if I call that run the turning point of my life. After a few questions with the expert, the image was finally lucid.

We slowly left her office, walked to the tram station to ride back to the gray bag, the empty blue one, and all the rest. The tram was almost empty, the autumn sun was shining through the windows. It was a peculiar moment, the picture had now become vivid: I must go to the airport. The plans had to switch again by taking the plane that I hadn't yet missed.

Now it was only a matter of time to actually make it happen. It was a tornado of running around, rushing things through to get to the airport before my flight left the ground. I was again going back to the city that I took the train from in the morning, it was the return of the return trip. All these trips back & forth might confuse you, do believe me, I'm just as puzzled.

Nothing was important, the bags, the clothes, all the little things that I used to put on my working table. Not even the gray bag itself. I only had to make it to the airport, where, I was then waiting in line with some trash in my hands, & a passport in my pocket to get stamped to legally leave the country. An important stamp, it should never be underestimated. Moving about without it is almost impossible. It's just as equally absurd when you see things from a bird's view. I would still fly in the same continent, it would still be in the same piece of land. Why would you even need a piece of paper, ink, & the stamp?! They are all dry surfaces of the Earth, with bodies of water in between. And we're only humans.

There were two gates to get the passports checked. I happened to queue at the one that was stuck. Isn't that always the way it is?! I stuffed the trash back in my pockets, hugged my hands and arms holding the belt of the funky red around my waist; the belt itself is one of the reasons why the bag is so funky. The officer had an issue with a passenger's documents, he was explaining things to them, or perhaps was asking them questions; I couldn't hear anything. I had to take a look at my passport. Nothing was wrong with my documents, but I couldn't help being concerned. The anxiousness must be for the passport I was holding, where I was born, or was coming from. You worry about things, even if everything is alright. There's a difference between humans, we're not the same. It's simple, the difference between you and me; one better than the other.

I closed my passport, & held it in between my palms. There was nothing to worry about; I checked twice. I'd already dropped the blue bag at the check-in counter; the black rucksack was resting calmly within. Honestly thinking, the last few weeks had been so rocky that only a vacation would put me back to myself. No diets, or very long runs. Our world was collapsing before our eyes, our very own village. So much bad news! It was equivalent to a person's lifetime supply of bad news broadcasted within a couple years. A family, or a large group of people. None of which mattered in the end, we would get used to it, each year more than the last, because it is only getting worse.

I could smile, & be happy for I was at the airport. Everything was alright, I almost had everything with me. If I'd thought faster, and started the action more quickly, I would've been able to bring the gray bag with. Some things, however, have a different ending. I was glad that I would take my seat in less than an hour. We would take off and fly into the open air, above the ocean of the still clouds, some of which might be rainy and stormy underneath. Though we wouldn't feel anything from above the clouds; safe and sound. We would swimmingly glide over the ninth wave that was about to hit. The tray of the food served onboard took over my thoughts, hurt my stomach, & made me wonder what was on the menu. I would take my time to eat it, I was not hungry, not even a small bit; I just had a huge salad. I would eat it as my cheesecake, enjoy the tasteless airplane food which I happen to like quite a lot. I could watch a movie with a glass of wine, or two, maybe even three, & four if I fancied. Well, I could, & I probably would; this flight hadn't come easy.

My boarding pass slid through my passport, & fell on the floor. I bent over to pick it up, very careful not to put pressure on my right knee. I wondered where my seat would be on this flight. I always asked the agent at the check-in counter to place me by the window. I'd first greet them, ask how they are, or how their day had been so far. If it's early in the morning, I would ask about their shift, how long they'd be working for. Then I'd ask them nicely if they could give me a window seat. They always say they'd check, & would set me by the window if there's an available seat. Some of them could even tell what I'm about to ask before I could speak it. And almost every time they set me by the window, except if there are no window seats available, or if they wouldn't be able to issue the boarding pass for the next one. I would appreciate their help, & thank them dearly. This must be the whole point of this invention, to fly, to float, to watch the Earth underneath.

For this trip, however, I didn't bother asking. I was the last one to check in, what was the point of asking when I knew the answer, other than just having a simple conversation? I could've asked the flight attendant to kindly ask another passenger if they'd like to swap seats with me. But I didn't see that happening either. I needed the window view the most, but I was out of energy to make an effort, or struggle a minute for it. I needed to comfort my eyes with beautiful images, to remind me that we're such small creatures in the grand scheme of things. To be mesmerized by the size of the mountains, towns, and villages as small as my fingertips. How many more of these corners are we missing?! It should be our right to step on different parts of the planet, wherever we fancied whenever. Get on the bus, train, bike, plane, or walk if you may. There's so much beauty that we're eliminated from, in a way, we're not allowed to see. In fact, we're guarded against them. Somehow like a prison, only, the other way around.

   I didn't ask for a window seat this time. And the passenger sitting by me by the window, simply shut the drapes all throughout the flight, which made me wonder why he even sat by the window in the first place. To lean his head against the wall?! He certainly had his own reasons, but it seemed like a huge waste of space. Perhaps he wasn't aware of how precious the spot he was holding was. It's as though someone would keep buying new clothes when their closet is loaded with beautiful outfits. Or when they keep buying food when the fridge is full. Or when someone doesn't enjoy the party, & keeps calling it boring. They probably don't know much about poverty, or what the hunger tastes like; maybe they haven't been lonely.

Eleven?!

The ferry was quite busy. It was the rush hour in the City, it was busy everywhere. I was walking fast, finding my way amongst other people getting inside the ferry. I was looking forward to grabbing myself a seat by the window. There was not much of a point in sitting by the window at that moment: the sun had already sunk, & it was dark outside; there wasn't much to see. It would only give me some privacy by keeping one side non-human. I could turn around to face the window and the wall which the glasses were framed in, to drift in my corner uninterrupted, pretend that I was seeing something out the window.

If I was in good condition, I would climb up to the second floor to have a better view of the dark strait we were passing through; it never gets old, always splendid, even though I've crossed it over for more than one hundred times. My right knee was still in pain, I was careful not to put pressure on it. It was already a lot of pressure on it. I was climbing uphill, stepping downhill, going places in the City through the alleys and back streets, & the shortcuts that we kept discovering.

I should've seen a doctor. I actually could've gotten myself checked out a couple weeks before when I was visiting my parents, but for some unknown reason, I didn't. I postponed it for later, which happened to be never. Hospitals are out of my patience. They smell funny, they're full of ill people. It's also very time consuming, going to the hospital I mean, it takes half of the day. Unless you go to a private hospital where you're treated like a valuable person for all the money you pay. Public or private, I don't think I'd be able to afford to visit a doctor either way. I can't really remember the last time I had health insurance. Well, I always have some kind of health insurance during my travels. It's one of the documents that cannot be missing to make the trip possible; it's a part of the legal procedure. But, that insurance would only cover for the emergency cases. If I broke my knee all of a sudden. Or if I was poisoned by food. It wouldn't cover the whole cost of the services or the medication, just partially; it would still be way off my very limited budget. I was living a life where getting sick was not really an option; I must've been so distracted to let myself get in such a terrible condition.

The ferry was an old one, not one of those newer versions that I liked. I couldn't really be so mad at the old ferries either. They would squeak with the waves, which somehow would drive you back to nostalgic memories, as if you're traveling in the past. Besides, it was only a thirty-minute ride, it would be over before you knew it. I found myself a seat on the far left corner by the small windows. There was a small radiator which was glowing heat gently. It was perfect, I couldn't ask for more.

I put the blue bag on my lap, now completely empty. I had to investigate the broken belt more in detail. It was damaged, in urgent need to be repaired. It looked like it was a totally different bag now that it was all empty. I'd left my things in a corner of Sahan's house to be able to carry the bag around with me, hopefully fix it in a way. It only felt funny to have the bag empty and be out with it.

If it's the case of a long trip, loading up would be a great concern, filling it up with excellent attention to make sure that every spot is occupied effectively. No space could be wasted with the wrong folding, or misplaced items. The order of the placement is quite important, heavier and bigger things go first; they'd better sit on the bottom of the bag. Then, the smaller pieces would fill in the gaps. Every little space counts: inside of the shoes, or inside of the thermos mug if you happen to carry one with you. Fragile things would be wrapped around clothes. The shirts cannot be wrinkled when you fold them in; they would only take more space. I personally roll most of my outfits, except if they're hefty winter wears. Specific items go into the side pockets, as if it's another drawer of the closet. Although, the curious thing with the blue bag was that it doesn't have any side pockets. It's just a large sack with a lid pocket on top, & an inner division on the bottom, to perhaps place the sleeping bag.

On the contrary, unloading wouldn't take much time or attention. The overall plan of the set up in the new environment had already been developed during the packing, why I'm taking what I'm taking. Things need to be sifted through before they get a pass inside the luggage. I've loaded my bags for quite a lot of times that it had somehow become a ritual, some kind of therapeutically satisfying routine; some type of reaction as soon as I see a piece of baggage. Standing on the other side of the line, holding an empty bag certainly felt unusual. Absurd, in a way. It reminded me of summer, light and easy, & that it wouldn't last very long; the bag had to be filled again soon.

There was something cheerful about its emptiness, can't quite tell what went through my mind, I just remembered the joy. It was the same notion when I finally emptied the black suitcase. The suitcase had to stay at Ömer's, a friend of mine, after I effectively broke the wheel. It was sad that it had to retire so early in its career. It was still rather functional by holding my valuable stuff for me till I returned. It was protecting the things that I couldn't travel with, nor could I discard instantly. It was only a matter of time to help me shred again, lose one more layer whenever I visited the suitcase. The black suitcase was big enough to patiently hold everything, all of the leftover stuff, as well as a huge spot on the back of my mind to have me worried about it every now and again; what was it like to wait in the corner of the storage room?! Funny how soon we forget our belongings once they're out of sight. Opening the suitcase was always a big surprise, to see my things, & remember the history for a brief moment. In the end, things magically got sorted, & the black suitcase was empty.

It made me a bit depressed to see the belt of the bag in such a terrible condition. Earlier in the day, I took it to a sofa tailor, thinking that they had advanced sewing machines to fix my problem. I realized that the issue was far more serious when the tailor said that he couldn't fix it. He only took a glance at it from behind his working station, and was very confident in his analogy. Then, I took it to the shoe repair store that I knew in our old neighborhood. I had visited the store with Vaid a couple of times, & met the guy who owned the shop. He was very skillful, quite dedicated to his job; I trusted him the most. He rejected the poor bag too, but he explained the reason why he couldn't fix it. There was a hard plastic sheet in between the soft sponges of the belt; the sewing machine would not be able to stitch through the plastic. Hopeless as one could ever be, I took it to another tailor on the way to the ferry station to measure the depth of the disaster. She said that she couldn't fix it either, which wasn't a surprise anymore, but she suggested hand-sewing it. She gave me the address to a thread shop not so far away. I hurried to the shop with a huge empty bag on my shoulder in order to find the right material to fix the broken belt.

The belt got dislocated a few days before, as I was on my way to Sahan's house from the airport. The bag was sitting on my back as heavy as it could be. The belt was wrapped around my waist to supposedly distribute the load evenly on my person, & to take the pressure off my shoulders. I might've wrapped the belt a bit too tightly, or pulled the bag a bit too strongly on my way off the super busy bus; it was stuck amongst the crowd. I heard the stitches tear as I stepped down. The belt was hanging loosely from the side when I reached the street, so I had to carry it on my shoulders for the rest of the way.

Well, it was only my fault, & I was the only one to blame. I wish I could put the blame on the people of the bus who didn't clear out the way, however, I was fully aware of what was going on inside the bag, & how come it was so hefty. Other than a few winter clothes which were more than enough for the whole while, & the materials that I couldn't sacrifice in the name of work, I had packed some food with me. Not the survival kind of food, some local ingredients that couldn't be found elsewhere. I was only thinking logically, it was simple math. Carrying them around with me would not only help my very limited budget, even only a small amount, they would indeed buy me the pleasure of eating tasty food in the future. It was rather an investment in time. I was in peace with my heavy luggage, had already accepted the fact. I had my reasons to bear the discomfort, the pain on the back, or on the knees, & struggling disastrously underneath the loads. Reminding me of the thought of home would be a proper pay-off; home is where. Only, I could've been more considerate of the unfortunate blue bag that had to hold an infinite number of items together. That was, yet, another moment for me to learn a valuable lesson, but I don't think I ever did.

I examined the belt from different sides and angles. It sure didn't seem like an easy piece to put together. No clue how I was supposed to stitch it back to the main body, though it had to be done. I had to start from somewhere; all my things were waiting to be placed neatly in the backpack. Nobody else took responsibility for the dislocated belt, it all depended on me. I started sewing. My hypothesis was to stitch it from every side, make them nice and tight so that the belt would remain attached. It wasn't easy, I have to admit, it was hard work. It required physical powers and lots of energy which I had highly underestimated. I cracked a sweat after a couple of minutes. I had no scissors, & the threat was thick. I was very cautious with the stitches, very careful not to make a wrong move; there was no going back to my quick fix.

The empty body of the bag was resting helplessly on my lap and the corner of my seat. I was facing the window, would raise my head to glance at the darkness behind the glasses every few stitches. The sound of the music was all over the room, played by some young musicians looking for financial support from the passengers of the ferry. It was somehow unfortunate that I never really had much to chip in. Nothing fancy, just a few coins would've been enough contribution. The money in my pocket was always too little that it was rather embarrassing to donate. It felt more like an insult to the band. Honestly thinking, I usually wouldn't feel so supportive of them. There were only a few occasions that the band was actually good, & I literally enjoyed the music. Sometimes they played horribly. I would've changed the channel if the radio in the living room was broadcasting it, in the kitchen, or the bedroom; you have no other choice when you're on the ferry. Although, fixing the cut belt was so confusing that I was almost completely detached; I'd stopped hearing the music.

It wasn't any of my concern if anyone was looking at me, whether or not they were judging me for the operation I was performing. It seemed more as a type of behavior from more dysfunctional members of the society, rather flawed, perhaps a misfit. And that was totally okay. I believe it was Ellen's description as she was commenting on situations as such, & the people like herself. Well, of course, she has a broader perspective of life; she's about fifty years older than me. It's always respectable to hear the opinion of an older person, even if they're only a year older, or two, let alone fifty years. Ellen believed some people were born as misfits. And according to her, we tend to go off-road, we take paths less stepped. She described it very beautifully, it was nice to listen to her. We met a few years back in the City during one of my annual visits. I introduced her to certain places, took her where I thought she might appreciate. Wait a second! Her name wasn't Ellen, I'm making a mistake here. Linda, oh yes, her name was Linda. How terrible I am with names! I believe I do have problems remembering them. I was actually discussing the matter with a group of new friends one summer's evening. Almost everyone else complained about the same issue; nobody claimed to be good at it. That was rather comforting to know we suffer the same, but mostly sad to see nobody could remember our names. We could be a bunch of nameless people to each other who had crossed paths, had made an impression to be collected in one place for the rest of the night, but would absolutely remain anonymous all the way till morning, because a name would take too much to remember. After a certain point, we would be too shy to ask for the names again, & admit that we have forgotten them just about when we heard them. That's the simplest way to show affection, in my opinion, to call each other by name. Later that evening, in between the exciting talks and curious conversations, a friend stated that the brain has the capacity to hold a certain number of names, so you'd forget a name as soon as you meet someone new.

I stretched my neck since I had held my head down on the bag all the while. It needed a few more loops with my big needle, & a decent knot by the end to call it done. We were about to arrive, I had to wrap the operation to leave it for later.

   As I was fixing the bag ready for a fast walk downtown, I looked around the room out of curiosity, to see what the crowd was doing on the ferry. Most people were scrolling down their phones if not all of them.

Less Than Ten

The winter had already arrived, even though it was yet autumn on the calendar. The trees were naked, the branches were bare, colors were lost. The wind was cold. The time to wear more layers had come; a jumper alone was not enough anymore. Looking out the windshield, the landscape was mainly in the color of brown, different shades of it. Yet, the stillness was graceful; nature never fails to be charming. Winter came early, left later than ever; that's how it's going to be from now on, it should be considered as the new normal as it already is for small children.

The seasons are swapping places just so gradually. It wouldn't be so surprising to wake up one of these days, & found the world close to its end. We were told about such days back in school. The world has an age, it would die someday, & we'd be left with a lifeless planet. There will come the day, we were taught, when the Earth as we know it wouldn't exist anymore. There would be different descriptions for the seas and the oceans and the landscape depending on which class it was, science or religion, or which subject was being taught. Regardless, they were all disastrous endings. People would have to keep moving in order to find safe grounds. I expected frenzied chaos, then. But rather, logically thinking, it would still be fine. The Earth had shifted slowly enough that things are well adapted to the madness. There should be a beginning, a certain number of years where the first odd behaviors took place. Not so dissimilar to our days; rain, storm, blizzard, the very hot sun for a few days before the forests went on fire. And a mysterious disease to wipe off all hopes from the face of the humans. People would already know how to respond; they've been wearing face masks for some time.

Religiously thinking, once the universe is faced with specific signs, it would end all of a sudden. As if it was coded with certain phrases to react with, and have the world end. The teacher would mention the signs as the increasing population of sinful people. Or, when the sadness rules, and there are no hopes. There, we've reached the apocalypse.

I used to get very nervous about all of this back in the school. I preferred hearing my parents' tales from the golden past when they were so young. I loved to hear how everything was different, more charming, comforting, & familiar. The future pictured in our school wasn't all very appealing. But the teacher would calm us down, reassure us that these would happen in a faraway future, & none of this would catch us any time soon; no need to worry about a thing. Today is the future. And we're not even driving flying cars. We're only left with bizarre winters, long and cold. On the other corner, people are preparing for the annual hurricane. The drought, lands being washed away with the flood, the houses, the cars.

It had been a long while, I really couldn't recall the last time I'd seen the blue sky; it'd been cloudy all the way. The clouds were fat and gray. Giant, there didn't seem to be an end. It wasn't going to rain, it wasn't cold enough to make it frost either. The scarce sun made the times even more gloomy. The landscape was about to fall asleep.

It was a good moment to slow down, tuck into the cave, ponder a bit more. Work more intensely now that there wasn't much more to it; the landscape was brown. Perhaps to speak with the inner self, remember to smile more often, and untie the frown upon the forehead. As cheesy as it sounds, it was time to see life for what it was, to find the beauty in bareness. The sunglasses were set aside, we were out of ingredients to caramelize the top.

We were driving to the south to connect to the main road to the east. We were moving toward the south-east. I had been moving a lot. Most of my days were on the road; I only moved forward. Watched the landscape, perhaps gained new perspectives on the go. Packing was the new skill that I tried to master in order to get by more efficiently. Within a couple weeks, it appeared that only a few pieces of clothes is more than enough; you'd been wearing the same things over and over. And if they're all about the same color, you save so much time doing laundries, as well as maintaining a fashionable style easily. The only thing you must be mindful of is personal health, really. Gaining weight is something to avoid at all costs. Bigger size means bigger clothes; it means more fabric, more space occupied in the bag, more weight on the shoulder, even by only few grams. Injuries are not welcomed, they just hold you back which is against the whole idea of being on the road, of moving forward. I taught myself a couple of tricks to be without labels, good or bad, painful, memorable, eye-opening, or sometimes heart-breaking. The expectations had to remain as low as zero.

In my head, the road has always been another word for freedom. If the main road ends, side roads and back roads begin, then comes the footpaths & dirt paths. The road can lead you to an infinite number of places, anywhere you can imagine, or cannot. I'd already realized I didn't have much of it, the freedom I mean, the end was within easy reach. There were lines to close my road; going further always calls for permissions. The natural flow of things is killed when the road is interrupted, when the freedom is broken. Freedom, of course, comes in many forms and shapes and conditions. The money in your pocket, the pigments on your skin, the shape of your eyes, the ring on your finger. We're absolutely free beings. Nothing can stop us from listening to birds and chasing them in the sky, watch the clouds and call them by their names. To take a walk, watch the houses, how the doors and the windows look because every one of them is supposed to be different.

You don't need to have much to enjoy a picnic around the neighborhood. But it does get frustrating to know that you have to come up with a reason, a series of arguments to defend yourself in order to have a sandwich for lunch in the other park across the imaginary drawn lines. Perhaps you didn't want to go all that far to begin with, perhaps the bliss of the slim tree would've been enough for your party; you just would want to visit the park out of curiosity, a change of pace from the ordinary. The sandwich gets stuck in the throat once you know you can't go beyond, once you know the freedom is gone.

Who's to blame, then, if a young student needs to use the bathroom in the middle of the lesson, but cannot, as long as the teacher wouldn't allow it during the class. The bathroom is there, perhaps less than ten steps away by the end of the hall, & the young child wets their pants since they cannot reach it. The disaster has happened, & the damage is done. Who's to blame?

The teacher, or the manager who sets rules for the school?! Or perhaps it was the kid's fault with all the bad timing.

It had been an hour since we'd left the house. By that point, we'd almost reached the highway. The initial plan was to leave early in the morning, but we were pleased that we could eventually leave before noon. We had a car; the plans could stretch as long as we fancied. Such a great privilege, it's my greatest wish to own one. It's another word for freedom, why not taking advantage of it as long as you have it?!

The pressure is off certain elements of the trip, the car would take care of them for you: the weight of your load, for instance, or the things that won't fit in your small suitcase. The car could potentially be your bedroom if the events left you without a home. Certainly, there are other things to worry about when you've got the car. If there's enough fuel, whether or not the engine is in good condition, if the tires are strong enough for the frozen roads.

We put our bags and the rest of our stuff in the trunk of the car. I put the black rucksack on the backseat. And the basket of food and snacks within reach, & placed the tea flask in between the driver's seat and the co-pilot's. I glanced one last time around the house to make sure that it's tidied up and clean, & nothing was being left behind. Hugged my father goodbye. We were going to meet up again soon, less than ten days, yet, it wasn't any less sad. Tears may get involved, shaky voices, hanging lips, and frowns in between the forehead. We left.

For the first time in a long while, I didn't have to worry much. It was nice to just get in the car, and drive for hours in our personal space. The only thing left to do would be to enjoy the ride. The destination was known, the food was ready, & there was enough money in the pocket to protect us from any unwished surprises. It was all taken care of.

We had already been warned about the condition of the road we were going to take before we reached the highway. Certain parts of it were under construction. And that we might want to take another route, which would take us a bit longer, but surely would've been an easier ride. I preferred the usual path; I was used to it, & I knew the directions so we wouldn't get confused, or even lost. First, we'd pass through the countryside, running amongst the farmlands and small villages. Some towns and factories in between. Then slowly bigger towns would show up before we reached the highway.

Whenever we passed it by, it was a different time of the year, different seasons with different colors. It was the same landscape, but not quite the same. I watched the view with all my attention. I feared I might be losing something in the end.

We stopped in the town before we turned into the highway. The town was famous for its butter bread, which was too delicious to pass by. I can't really remember the last time I had them, even then, I had no intention of buying any, not even as a fresh tasty souvenir.

I'd traveled through that route for so many times that I almost knew every bit of it, I could tell what was about to come with my eyes closed. The part that I loved the most was not all that far away. There are certain bits that I enjoy better than the rest. There's something about them that catches my attention in a way that I can't let go, even if I pass them hundreds of times. It could be anything, the dense forest of the valley awaiting by the end of the tunnel, the turns of the road over the edge of a cliff, or the smallness of the town by the sea from the top of the mountain. Perhaps there's something in them to relate to, something captivating depending on where my stream of thoughts float about. It also depends on my emotional state of being to make that moment linger on. It's something to look forward to if I'm lucky enough to travel along that way once again. The first trip is a big surprise. But as the pureness of the early excitement vanishes, the rest becomes noticeable. You observe things which would make you wonder if they'd been there all along.

We were about to reach the part where I savored the most. A valley of colorful mountains was worth nothing but all the attention. They looked like a layered sponge cake set in different forms and directions; each layer had a distinct color. The colors were bright and pronounced, quite unique with a specific name. But not as bold as few drops of food coloring inside the cake batter. Maybe the red was for half a cup of cherry juice, the yellow for a spoon full of saffron, or some cocoa and coffee to make the brown. The colors would be more hypnotizing when you take a walk on one of those hills, realize the individual stones don't even carry the colors seen from the distance.

Twelve Hours

Someone was kneeling on my legs. I pulled down my jacket off the head to investigate the situation. There was a man on my legs, a fully grown man who had put his knee on me with half of his weight. He was leaning on the back of the plastic bench, calling out his child. There was a small playground behind the bench where the kids were playing. I guess his child was one of the naughty loud kids jumping up and down on the spongy well in the middle, screaming and having a blast. The father was asking him to behave, calm down, come to them for lunch, or something to that sense as far as I understood; he was speaking a different language.

I tried to move, did my best to get up. Quite unsuccessful indeed, I gave it another shot. Nothing was accomplished; I couldn't even move a knuckle. I was as heavy as a rock in the middle of the river, but I think I lifted up my head about enough to let the man know that there was a person underneath the pile of black clothes: black jacket and the black cargo trousers; I was not a traveling bag. He immediately understood, perhaps he already felt the humanness of the surface underneath his leg. He apologized, and apologized; he was awfully embarrassed about it, so he apologized again, & showed his both palms to me, his fingertips pointing to the sky, to tell me how sorry he was. I smiled, saying silently that it was alright, that I could see it was an honest mistake.

I let my head fall back on the black rucksack with my eyes open. I starred at the ceiling. It was high. There were so many poles flying in every direction that were connecting different columns and bigger poles. They were making such curios geometrical shapes. I followed the lines, slide my eyes in the space in between them. Many different shapes that I could recognize or not, some of which surely had a specific name. The noises in the background didn't seem to ever stop. I left my ears on them as I kept my gaze softly on the ceiling. Let the brain empty, I was up from hazy dreams.

A pre-recorded voice was announcing the flights, asking the passengers to go to their gates. I could hear the howling of the airplanes beyond the soundproof double-shield windows as they took off. It was almost dark outside. It was snowing. I gave myself a minute before I could raise my left arm to check the time. I was not in a hurry, I was only curious. The layover was about twelve hours, and my passport wouldn't allow me to leave the airport; there certainly was loads of time left before I had to get to my gate.

I'd walked up and down the hallway a few times to be able to find the right spot to plug in my computer. It could be considered as an afternoon walk, even though the conditions weren't quite perfect; the bag was heavy, my knee hadn't fully recovered yet, so every step was a pain. But the walking would help digest the super healthy lunch I'd packed for myself, & hopefully would loosen up my tight muscles on the legs which hadn't worked throughout. I sat on the carpeted floor, leaned my back against the bag I'd put by the column, & plugged in my computer. Some people, I noticed, were sitting on the bare floor. I couldn't understand how someone possibly would sit on the stones in the dead of winter; it was out of my comprehension. The floor was cold, did they not feel that?! How come they wouldn't sit on the carpet as long as they had the chance to?! Why suffer whilst the comfort was in front of them?!

I pushed the button on the top left corner of the computer to turn it on, & waited for the system to load. The airport was now quite busy, full of passengers of any kind, travelers going everywhere. The pre-recorded voice was constantly announcing flights to different directions. I was keeping track of the information that I didn't need at all. It was the sound of a woman. She was very calm, neutral without any emotions; she sounded very strong. She would've sounded different if you spoke with her on a usual day, but she sounded more as a machine, perhaps it was for the speakers of the airport, or the critical information she was sharing.

There was another announcer that you'd hear every now and then which would speak through a microphone live from the airport, probably from the general office or a booth upstairs. The announcers would be different every time. They sounded as if they were in a hurry, speaking through the microphone in between getting the rest of the work done. They were calling for certain passengers to hurry, for the airplane would take off soon, otherwise, they would have to leave without them. If they didn't show up on time, the airport crew had to unload their luggage, which is not really the most fun job; they'd have to go through all the suitcases of the passengers on board to find the correct one, take it to the lost and found office, & inform the passenger about the situation; they might as well wait a few more minutes for the passengers to show up; they're for sure somewhere within the airport.

The names sounded funny when they were being pronounced. I could tell that some of them were foreign names to the announcer. The pronunciations were wrong; how would they know?! My name would've been impossible. Not even my fellow-citizens could say it properly, let alone foreigners. I tried to remember if I'd ever been announced at any airport, then I thought about it for a moment. I couldn't remember anything. I usually get to the airport early, & I wait at the gate even before it's open. As a matter of fact, I quite like arriving at the airport early, helps me tune in with the trip. I usually take a nap at the gate because I'm tired almost before any trip. I tend to leave all the packing, cleaning, potential shopping, sometimes visiting the post office, or any type of work that needs to be done before traveling to the last minute. So, everything is squeezed in only a few hours; a lot needs to be done, it's not a mystery why I'm so tired all the time.

But then, after a moment of thinking, I remembered my name had actually been announced on a couple occasions. The first one was way back, almost ten years before. I ran into a friend who was taking the same flight as I was. We went downstairs to get some coffee in one of the over-priced cafés. The conversation, whatever it was about, stretched long, in a way that we entirely forgot about the clock, the flight, our suitcases. We almost missed the plane. We got on board, looked up our seat numbers under the heavy looks of the flight attendants. The fuming faces of other passengers as we sat down was indeed remarkable. They were questioning us without words, judging us silently, asking what we were up to, & what took us so long.

The second incident wasn't actually very far away. I was on my way to the City for a short visit, & pick up some clothes from the black suitcase. In order to maintain my very limited budget,

I'd managed to buy an inexpensive ticket, perhaps the cheapest flight one could ever get. Even though it wasn't the longest airport trip ever, it felt like an eternity; a total of two layovers and three airplanes. The extensive waiting hours in between had made it impossible to stay conscious, & as we all know by now, the airport naps wouldn't really recharge the brain very well. My mind was wandering aimlessly in the images it was generating of the near future, meeting friends after such a long time, and sleeping for twelve hours.

I was so far gone that I didn't notice how I possibly left my wallet at the check-in counter. I didn't realize it was missing out of my pocket until I realized that a cup of coffee was the only way to stay alert, & most probably alive. I went to a café, reached for my wallet in the left bottom pocket of my cargo trousers as I walked to the cash register. But, it wasn't there; the wallet was missing. I checked all my pockets for about three times just in case I'd put it somewhere other than its usual place; it wasn't in any of the pockets. I panicked, of course. I ran back the path walked to find the lost one. The good thing was that I realized its absence at the right time. I scanned all over the airport, checked every corner and spot that my foggy brain recalled being to since the gorgeous wallet was last seen. I was led to different security points. One question led to another, I eventually ended up in lost and found office. The agent gave me a sharp look from the top of his glasses, asked me where I was all the while, & how come I didn't react when they announced my name for sixteen thousand times. I told him that I didn't notice; I honestly didn't. They might've pronounced it in a funny way which was not relatable to me on any level.

Speaking of which, I couldn't stop thinking about coffee. I could smell it, feel the hot cup in the palm of my hands. I wouldn't spoil the drink with milk or sugar, not even a cookie, or a square of dark chocolate; it was just about coffee. It was that time of the day where you'd enjoy a break on the couch of the living room. A cup of black tea would work just fine, which had been steeping in the teapot over the boiling water long enough to extract all the essence out of the roasted leaves; a very casual late afternoon on a winter's day in my agenda.

All I did, however, was take a few deep breaths to let go of the urge, & remind myself that a cup of coffee at the airport was way off my budget; times were hard. I took a big sip of the water out of my blue bottle which I'd filled up from the tap in the restroom. I tried to stay focused on the work on my lap that had to be finished. It wasn't so much about the place to trigger the action, I'd begun to notice, it was mostly about the time. Time to sleep, time to work, or to eat. Time to drink coffee, or to start the party; it could be anywhere as long as you feel what you're supposed to. If the surface is comfortable enough to bring good dreams, it could be called the bed. I was at the airport, at its busiest time, yet the work was flowing like water down the river. Concentrating might be a challenge, which could be overcome by practice. Doing anything continuously would turn them into a habit; this too can be perfected. Aren't we all a bunch of live habits in the end?! Things that we do over and over, again and again.

The airport was large enough to provide anything I'd ask for; I had to remain there for a while. As if it was home for half a day. I had many options to locate the bedroom, the dining room, & the studio to finish off the work that was about to meet the deadline. I could pick the south or the north view as the ideal one to wake up to. I would place my couch somewhere I could see the sky as I looked up; the perfect home in my dictionary, the one that would show you the sky whenever you fancied.

I lifted my left arm to check the time, even though the hall was full of clocks. There was still plenty of time. The gate was still closed, but the suitcases must've been transferred to the airplane by then. I couldn't help worrying if my luggage would go missing again. I highly doubted that I would be that misfortunate to lose my luggage twice, but there was always a chance. This time getting the load back would've been a serious issue; I really didn't know where I was going. I only knew the name of the village, which I couldn't really pronounce. I didn't have any address, or any information about the location I was going to be residing. I didn't even know what it was going to look like. I'd spoken with the owners, Domas and Eglė, but we had discussed other topics. The house was going to be a big surprise, or rather, a mystery.

It was going to be a big headache if my blue backpack went missing in between the flights, or if anything else happened for that matter. The airport crews weren't really careful with the suitcases as they were transferring them into the airplane as far as I'd noticed. They would toss and throw them with about zero concern. And that's only the part we see, who knows what goes on inside the plane once we take off. Suitcases don't have seatbelts; nothing secures them in any way.

I was mainly anxious about the belt of the blue bag that was recently broken. It was nicely sewed back to its place in the end; I'd done my best, I believe I could call it a success. Though I'm no professional, no idea how a broken belt is supposed to be fixed. As I was handing the backpack over at the first check-in counter, I tucked in the shoulder straps and the belt to fully zip up the back cover. Then, wrapped the bag in its raincoat, & sealed it with the handy blue belt. The belt was supposed to provide a practical & obvious handle for the airport crew so they'd lift my heavy load easily without harming it.

I'd packed in such a great hurry, I couldn't remember what was where inside the bag. By that point, I wasn't so sure why the bag was so heavy anymore, what it was so important that I had to take with me. There wasn't anything that I couldn't live without. Realistically thinking, it was going to be a long trip where everything was unknown; I'd packed everything I'd thought I might potentially need. Anything that would've helped with the budget, or eased the new world I was about to dive into, to make the unknown more familiar.

I shut the lid of my laptop. The work was done. I was wondering if I should move to another part of the airport, discover a bit more before I had to show up at my gate. A very short nap seemed to be a good idea now that the coffee was out of the picture. I put my laptop back in its place inside the black rucksack, realized once again how heavy it actually was as I set it up on my shoulders. I walked down the hallway, looking for a seat by the window. The sound of music reached me as I stepped forward. It was the beat of the drum, and an occasional ring on the bell; somebody started to sing. I walked closer to the sound. The sky was dark gray, & the white snowflakes were falling down weightlessly; some view to watch. The previous winter had passed by strangely. Perhaps that was the first winter that went by without the snow. Not that it was such a big deal, just a curious observation. It somehow felt like the whole year was one long rainy season, no snow to reset the calendar, & help us prepare for the spring. Little that I knew, it was only going to get stranger; summer without a swim, sun-bathing in mid-autumn, another snowless winter way up North, & many more to come.

Minus Thirteen

    Can't quite remember how many days it was, I must've noted it somewhere, but it was by far the longest I hadn't left the house. It was the mad blizzard that had locked me in. I'd attempted to leave the Cottage for a walk, even if it was a very short one; some fresh air would've been nice. Although, it was impossible; I only made it a couple steps out the front door. The storm was so brutal that it would cut through the skin. The giant waves of stormy clouds floating above were overloaded and aggressive; it didn't seem to be vanishing away soon. At some point during the lockdown, the storm slowed shortly; I heard a couple of birds chirping. But my windows were almost fully frozen to block me from having a look outside. Even though the blizzard had made life an absolute bore, I couldn't be so mad about it for its perfect timing all throughout. I was busy with a deadline during the storm, I had to stick to my table regardless. And it stopped in the evening prior to my trip. The clouds hadn't gone anywhere, they only stopped snowing, which was actually the perfect condition; they would act as a hefty blanket that would keep the warmth of the body within.

Arturas and I were supposed to be leaving in the morning. He'd asked me to be at the gate by eight o'clock. I'd prepared my stuff the night before so that I wouldn't forget anything. Not that I really took a whole lot with, the rucksack was ready.

It was white everywhere; the whole scenery was covered in snow, the fields, the road, bushes and the naked trees. It felt adventurous to be the first one stepping on the snow, as if I was discovering an unknown land, somewhere untouched, somewhere that humans have not yet reached; sounds funny when I say so, a piece of land that hasn't yet been spoiled, as if such place even exists at all. Some say the whole world can be rediscovered by each individual separately, in other words, for seven billion times. They say it's a rather personal experience, the inner journey, or something to that sense.

I pulled the front door closed behind me, made sure that it was secured in its frame. The Cottage was over a hundred years old, different parts of it had gained consciousness and could react independently. I made the first step; the snow crushed underneath my boots. It was crisp, glittery, and dense. Slim layers created by the wind around the corners seemed very curious. I took a closer look for a few seconds. The snow was almost up to my knee which made walking a real challenge. It took me a very long time to finally reach the gate.

The car was parked a few steps away from the gate. The engine was running, it was humming a grim monotonous melody. As I walked to the car to take the co-pilot's seat, I noticed the door was open ajar; Arturas must've left it open for me. I hopped inside quickly, shut the door behind me before the freezing air entered the car any further; it was the coldest month of the winter, thankfully, we'd passed the coldest day. I said hello, smiled, & nodded to complete my greetings. He said hello, & greeted me warmly with a broad smile on his face. We didn't exchange any other words. There was no common language between the two of us, so verbal communication was down to almost zero. We usually had a friend with us who could translate, & connect us in a way. Sometimes it would be his daughter, sometimes we asked Domas for help.

   I put the bag down by my feet. It was a bit bloated for the extra sweater; space was a bit too small for it. I had to force it down a bit, push and wiggle it from side to side until it found its place. Arturas pointed to the bag, then to the backseat, meaning that there was some empty space in the back, & that I could put it there if I wished. Well, it was a bit too late to know that. I told him it was alright, the bag was not really making me uncomfortable. I was going to need something from it at some point during the trip, not too bad to have it nearby.

   It was also rather comforting to keep it within reach just in case something occurred, some kind of accident, or if the world ended all of a sudden. My friend Pel had planted this idea in my head a few years before. She was telling me about one of the things that intimidated her on a day to day basis. We were having tea, & it was later in the afternoon. She told me whenever she left the house, she would imagine the things she had with her might've been the only things she could ever have. An earthquake could always tear their house down, or some other catastrophe that we were too safe in the living room to think of. It was a very curious idea. Back then, her theory sounded peculiar, rather funny as a matter of fact. But, now, it's perfectly sensible. The stories that we were told during the forest fire weren't all that far away from what Pel had expressed as one of her biggest concerns.

   Arturas changed the gear to one. I fastened my seatbelt as he slowly drove away. I looked at the very small digital clock on the dashboard in between the radio and the heater which was gently blowing warm air into the room; I was late by two minutes. I'm always late, I don't really understand how it can happen. Regardless of all my efforts to make it on time, I would still be late. Even if it's only by a minute, I still manage to fall behind time. One minute is quite a long while. It's the difference between missing your flight, and flying away in the air. It's so long when you're waiting for a friend to arrive. There's a big disappointment when the expectations don't meet reality, when you excitedly arrive at the meeting point, and you don't find your friend there. You realize that you'd have to wait; every second would last as long as eternity.

I wanted to apologize to Arturas for my delay, but I couldn't find a proper way to express it without words. I thought of pointing to the clock, & coming up with some kind of hand or body gestures to motion how sorry I was about it, but none of my acts would be clear enough, & it would only get us more confused. So I decided to let go, & assume that being late for a couple minutes wasn't that big of a deal. I wouldn't really mind if a friend was late, I would wait at any rate. It would be slightly annoying to arrive and not to find them there, but I'd recover happily as soon as they'd turned up.

We passed by the small park in front of the glorious church in the center of the town. Or, should I call it the village?! He pointed to the bust in the middle of the park, then turned his finger to the church, & said that it was the sculpture of the architect of the building. I was fascinated to learn about it; I had passed them by all the while without realizing it. I was thankful to him for sharing the information, & mostly thrilled to understand his point. The lucky thing is that so many words have traveled freely between the languages. Sometimes it's the case of the words that have been invented recently, the ones that got popular before they could be translated, & found an equivalent for, such as sugar or coffee. In some cases, the words are for technological or modern devices, so the necessity of translation is not required as much. Everyone knows what television is. Sometimes, you don't need words to express the thoughts; things can speak for themselves. Offering food utters affection, handing a drink is a genuine welcome, & a dance invitation could be the first step of friendship.

We drove away and left the town. We were both sitting quietly as we were looking ahead. His eyes were locked on the road, mine were wandering about. There was a comfort in our silence; the road eased our way, softened the edges of the quietness. It was nice to sit by a friend and not speak. Not speaking should be a more common activity in our social interactions, I don't believe we do it enough. In the loud world of ours, it's a bit hard to imagine asking a friend out to exchange only few words during the meeting. People might think we're sad, or mad at each other. There must be a certain level of closeness between the two friends to enjoy the experience the best. However, there's no reason why it couldn't be practiced with new friends just as well, people who feel a connection on some level. All there is to do is to sit by one another, & not speak. In the living room, in a busy bar, perhaps in the studio, or in the park if the weather is pleasant, in a car driving by the frozen farmlands dressed in ice and snow.

It wasn't the first time I was catching a ride with Arturas, it sure was not going to be the last. It was quite generous of him to include me in his plans. He had invited me over to his house for a hot drink the first time we met, introduced me to his family, & showed me their home. A couple weeks after, I paid them a short visit around five in the afternoon; they made coffee, & offered me some local aged cheese. And the next time I knocked on their door was to get some help for Kirke when she was very ill. I might've told you the story, perhaps you'd recall; they weren't home. It didn't feel unfamiliar to sit in the car with him, & say nothing the whole ride through. We only exchanged a couple of words randomly. He would point out to certain things that he thought might interest me, an old school in a village, a factory in the distance, or an abandoned manor house; we fully understood each other in that sense.

And the silence would again rule the car. The landscape was always fascinating enough to fill in the gaps. The land was almost completely flat, rather similar looking all over. We would drive for minutes, yet it would all look the same, as if we hadn't gone anywhere. It was mainly farmlands wherever you'd look. Some pieces of forests would show up randomly, which we had to drive through on occasions, otherwise, I would keep watching them from afar. The hills, even though very short, were a nice touch to the flatness the road was passing by. As time went by, I discovered that the whole region was a wide flat land mainly dedicated to agriculture; it looked almost all alike wherever I went, north, east. Some areas were better known for their lakes, some for their pine tree forests, but the reputation was for the farmers. With the passage of time, and the gradual disappearance of winter, the true colors of the land showed up: yellow, reddish-brown, fresh green. They would keep changing almost every day; the difference would be dramatic if you somehow missed the landscape for about a week. Green would turn into yellow swiftly, or maybe, yellow to green. But for our silent ride, all there was to see was white and pale blue. Except for the road itself, & the signs right by it. Reading the names of the town and villages we were passing by was quite entertaining, keeping count on how far away we were from each, or how long it would take us to reach which.

We made it to the crossroad outside the town to connect to the main road. The road forked into three ways: left, right, and the path that carried on ahead. Different signs were pointing each way. On the side, I read the name of the town of our destination one syllable at a time, & got excited to see it so soon. Arturas smiled, & approved that it was indeed where we were headed. But he drove straight ahead instead. I was puzzled, though the confusion was all cleared as he switched the flasher on to the left, & drove to the gas station; we needed fuel. He went inside the store after he loaded the car, & started chatting with the lady behind the counter. They must've known each other; everybody knows one another in smaller towns.

All of a sudden, a familiar smell filled in my nose. Similar to fresh berries off the bush. It smelled red with a hint of black and purple. It was strong enough to take me back to old memories; scents and tastes are so intimate to have such power. You can identify the smell once you have some kind of history with it, some type of memory, or an experience that would let you name it. Smells carve memories. Once I had an accident with the fireplace in my Cottage, in a way that the whole place was filled with smoke. The smell remained inside for over a week. It reminded me of the forest fire every time I entered the place, reminded me of barbeques and picnics.

Unlike colors and sounds, smells and tastes don't really have names; they're usually called by the origin source. The smell could be the indicator of so many verities, & could reveal a lot: if the food is still good or not, if there's an attraction between certain people. It gives you almost everything you'd need to know about the place when you first step in. Sometimes people carry the smell of their home inside their cars, even inside their bags believe it or not. Identifying different smells is quite hard as long as you haven't heard it before. For instance, the smell of the house I resided during the first journey. It hit my nose deeply the very first second I stepped inside the enormous household, although, not so sure how I could put it into words. I would say it smelled like coffee, cinnamon buns, with a hint of nutmeg, & many different foods that had been cooked in the communal kitchen; not so sure how I could describe it really. It was a distinct aroma, perhaps from the cured salmon or the codfish, the small pouches and bottles left from the guests from around the globe who used to live there at some point. Or perhaps the accumulation of all the above over the years, plus the air that has been trapped inside for a few weeks already since it was too cold to keep the windows open; you wouldn't really dare so. Pel asked me about the smell as I was back from my first trip, as if she magically knew all about it; she had traveled to some of the neighboring countries. I was absolutely stunned when she asked about it. Quite surprising to know it was a common smell in the northern regions of the continent; most of the houses smelled so. Pel and I both knew what kind of smell we were talking about, only, we were lacking words to depict it.

I had noticed that the smell of places is not really broadly spoken, & it's not a popular topic. I was traveling to stay in the Cabin for a while. Since I was very excited about the trip, I learn about the area as much as I could in advance in order to be clear where I was going. I came across lots of information, images, videos, notes of other travelers. However, nothing was mentioned about the smell, not even a sentence. That was quite unexpected. The hot springs, which are the signature landmark all over the island, have a very distinct and pronounced sulfur smell. I had visited hot springs elsewhere, but perhaps I was too young to recall the scent. It smelled more leftover hard-boiled egg. It's quite a natural smell, totally normal, but takes a while to get used to.

For us, it was a funny smell. We couldn't stop laughing and joking about it with Yasi; she was visiting me to travel around the island together, perhaps I told you about it before. We certainly needed some time to get used to it. I was eager to be able to appreciate it the way the locals did. Alda and Jon, her husband, took us for a quick tour to introduce some of the astonishing places nearby, including some hot springs. Alda would walk through the steam, would take deep breaths, & by waving her hands in the steam, she would take as much of the smell into her nose as physically possible. It was quite hard to handle, rather unpleasant to be perfectly honest. It took me a couple of weeks to notice how comforting the smell actually was. I would often take a walk around the lake of the village, visit the hot spring in the corner, step on the boiling dark sands, & would bathe myself in the white warm steam. I would inhale as deeply as one ever could to get more of the smell for I knew I'd be gone soon.

I opened the door to see where the smell was coming from; it certainly was more pronounced. Such a tasty smell, it made me want to eat whatever it was carrying on. Not that I was hungry. I was rendering my brain to decide what it reminded me of, what it was to make it so familiar. I remembered an early winter's morning on the terrace of a bar, where I was standing alone next to a bunch of strangers smoking cherry-flavored cigarettes. It was the same smell, however, I was at the gas station, & there was nothing around me. I stepped out of the car to chase it better. I took a deep breath, exhaled, & watched my white breath vanishing gradually into the air. The smell was inside my nose, but I couldn't distinguish the source. I was only thinking about that dark cold morning.
Arturas was holding a newspaper in one hand, & was making the payment with his other hand. I took another deep breath. The very cold air had made the inside of my nose quite dry and stiff; it was at least minus thirteen degrees. I sat back inside the car, & shut the door behind me. The smell was already gone.

Fourteen Steps

It was a harshly windy morning. The sun would shine through the clouds as they moved about with the wind, but it would be blocked again for the clouds were brought back together. The wind was sharp. The flatness of the open lands enhanced the brutality of the wind; there was nothing to buffer it, reduce its speed, or soften it in any way.

But thankfully, it wasn't as cold anymore; the air smelled spring. The trees were slowly waking up. The smallest leaf buds had started to sprout on the dry branches of the trees and bushes. They bloomed overnight; I got up one morning and they were already there. The trees looked as if they were covered in a green silk shawl from the distance. Standing by the trees every morning, keeping a close eye on them was my newest hobby. Maybe I missed a day in between, the baby leaves were about two days old. The leaves would've needed more sun to grow. The spring had arrived, though, it wasn't yet warm enough. To my surprise, however, some flowers had started to appear here and there. In fact, I had my morning coffee by the young red tulip by the front door. She was sitting there alone, moving vigorously with the wind, dancing in every direction. I watched her for a few minutes. I would've watched her longer, but I had to leave, it was getting late.

The black rucksack was hanging on the left shoulder as I closed the front door. I struggled with it for a couple of minutes to have it sit properly in the doorframe. With the change in the temperature, I had to jiggle it differently to have it sit alright, so that it wouldn't remain open ajar. And it was windy, it sure would flap open at some point, & the door to enter the Cottage would be revealed to the public by the end of the hall. I gave it one last wiggle, realized it was taking too much of my precious time. I decided to leave it as it was; there was nobody there to see you wouldn't need a key to step inside.

I took my undergarment off the branch, & walked away from the door. I had reminded myself for sixteen thousand times to take it off the tree and put it in my bag before I left. But, I forgot. Luckily, the wind made it shake so madly that I noticed it on my way out, otherwise, it would've been blown away to the open fields in the end. I'd washed it earlier in the morning as I took a shower, it was completely dry by the time I was leaving. I'd assumed that it would still be a bit damp, but the warm sun and the wind had made a decent drier. I folded it carelessly to put it in my left pocket. There was no time to pause, take off the bag, fit it in, get the rucksack back on the shoulders again. My right hand was already occupied with the trash bag that I was planning to dump on my way to the bus stop.

The wind was so forceful that it was pushing me backward; every step was hard work. I was walking along the dirt path behind my Cottage. The path was dry, so were the fields around; it'd been quite a long while since it'd rained, which was very unusual for that area. It was dusty everywhere, the wind was making a big mess. No good condition. Lucky that I had my sunglasses on; they were at least letting me see where I was going.

I reached Zita's yard, my closest neighbor. Their dog, which was chained by their very small pond, started barking aggressively. That's what he would do whenever he saw me. I was wondering when he was going to recognize me. The dog was loud. And very mad. I was held up with my own thoughts and concerns that I didn't bother having a look at the furious dog. I would pass him by in a few seconds; he would calm down.

I walked by the yard. The bushes were shaking wildly behind the metal fences. The dog was still barking near me, even though their yard was almost left behind; it was getting further away with my quick steps. I looked around. Their small dog was walking very closely by my feet, and was barking his small guts out. He was very loud even in that noisy wind, and he was very small. I raised my voice to ask him to be quiet, to leave me alone. He was still very loud, & determined. I spoke to him even louder, asked him to let go, but he wasn't going anywhere. It was best to ignore him; he would probably return back to his home at some point. He didn't. He was distracting. I imagined that he couldn't hear me through the wind. I raised my voice once more. In a way, I was shouting. I tried to shush him. But there was no point. I believe he kept following me until I reached the road. He didn't care if he was off his territory.

I raised my left arm to check the time: it was very late. I picked up my pace, & hurried a bit more since I was about to miss the bus. Walking faster wasn't the easiest thing to do at that moment. It somehow felt like a dream in which you would try to run, mostly away from the monsters, but you wouldn't really be moving forward. The harder you try, the more trapped you'd feel, the more irritated you'd get. But this wasn't a dream, or a nightmare for that matter, & I wasn't going to wake up from it. The clock was ticking, more quickly than ever, yet I wasn't getting anywhere.

The trash bins started to appear up the road in front of the houses, different colors for different types of trash: brown, black, green, and blue. I had no idea which bin my trash belonged to. It was a plastic plate, which was lined with another type of plastic on the inside to secure the container from any potential leakage. There was another kind of plastic wrapped around the plastic plate to protect the food inside furthermore. There was also some paper attached to the wrapping which included the name of the food, the ingredients, the price, & the manufacturer. Ideally thinking, each part of my trash should've been tossed in a different bin; some of the materials were not recyclable anymore. But I decided that they were all considered recyclable plastic, they could all go into the blue bin, or was it green?!

I tried walking faster, the wind was not letting me do so. It was blowing so strongly, so sharp that it was hurting my skin. I tried walking backward, facing the part of the road that was left behind. In fairytales and bedtime stories I grew up with, for some mystical reason, it's told that you shouldn't look back the path you've walked by. It wasn't clear what was supposed to happen when you do look back, but, it's the last advice from the fairy, or the witch of the village given to the protagonist of the story. They were to keep on ahead their way, & never look back. Otherwise, it was all going to be a disaster. They might be referring to the metaphysical aspect of it, that the path left belongs to the past. And once it's past, it's not real anymore. You might get caught up in the illusion of something that is out of reach, something unreal. Things tend to feel better once they pass by. The agony is not sensible at any time except for the present. You don't quite remember how painful it was, or how intense; you don't remember the bitterness. Time changes the taste. I turned around to face forward again. Walking backward was only slowing me down if it was doing anything at all.

I reached the first trash bin which belonged to the neighbors living by the road. It was rather intimidating to use others' bin for some ridiculous reason, felt as if I was committing a crime. You never know what's illegal where. I glanced at the house to check if anyone was around to witness my act. I lifted the lid half-way to make sure my plastic plate belonged there. However, the bin was empty. The garbage truck must've gotten there before I did. Just to be sure, I checked few other bins in different colors, took a look into other neighbors' bins as well; they were all empty. If I had managed my time more properly, I could've thrown my trash in our bin on the other side of the yard by the barn. Or, I could've taken it to the main garbage disposals of the village which wasn't far off my way, but there wasn't much time left, & I had to hurry. I decided that I'd better give up on being a responsible citizen, and chuck the plastic plate in one of the small bins of the park in front of the church. The pressure would be off my shoulders, somebody else would need to take care of it from then.

There was no one at the bus stop when I arrived. It was the first time I was taking that bus, so I wasn't really familiar with the system, whether or not the stop was supposed to be that empty. Though, I had seen people waiting for the bus around the same hour as I passed it by during one of my long walks.

It was rather unusual to see it so. Not even a bag or a jacket as evidence that people were waiting, they'll be back for their thing. It was obvious that the bus was gone, & I had already missed it; whatever I did from then on in order to investigate the situation was utterly pointless, but I toured around to see if there were any other chances.

I looked for someone I could ask about it. Nobody, not even a single soul near our stop. Well, I wasn't really thinking logically at that point. Even if there was somebody, we wouldn't be able to speak a language in common. I raised my left arm and rolled up the sleeve to check the time; the bus was definitely gone. I had to improvise another way.

As for my last shot, to be certain that the trouble was real, I crossed the street to ask the woman who was selling goods on a small table by her car. The car was parked in the narrow shoulder by the post office, not so far away from the bus stop. Can't really call it a marketplace, it was only small parking space in front of the supermarket. Well, not really a supermarket; it was a small shop. But, different cars and trucks would stop by on each day of the week to sell their goods. I could never tell which day was for what, some days it would be second-hand clothes, some days it would be a meat truck selling sausage and cheese. It was quite unpredictable, just as you never knew when they would collect the trash.

This time, the shop was closer to the theme of a hardware store. There were all kinds of things on the table: scissors and ropes and glue. The lady was attending a costumer when I reached her, an older man who was buying something, a sponge, a button, or perhaps some papers. She was putting his things in a green plastic bag; I waited.

I kept my head to the left on the road in case the white bus showed up. The stop was only across the street, I could've reached in a few seconds. Even if I barely made it, which I highly doubted it would be the case, the driver would still see me running, would wait for me. If, only if the driver was nice enough. Once I missed the bus by only a second, I was less than fourteen steps away from the stop. The driver had obviously seen me with the gray backpack on my shoulders, dragging the brown suitcase wrapped in the blue belt behind me, yet, he drove away inhumanly.

The lady was chatting with the old man, counting the coins in the palm of her hand before giving them to him. I was really hopeful that the bus would show up. With the power of my gaze reflection upon the road, the bus had to magically come back, & get me out of this misery. Nothing was moving, really; it was only the clouds passing by, the leafless trees that were trembling about with the wind, crows and birds flying in the distance. The old man left with the green plastic bag.

I approached the lady who was now free to attend a new costumer. I said hello, & asked if the bus was gone already. I pointed to my watch, then to the bus stop across the street, & finally down the road to the left. She shrugged her shoulders, said that she couldn't understand the question. Of course she couldn't! I asked the same question again, but this time, I added the name of the neighboring town which the bus was headed to. I also motioned a car riding down the road with my hand and arm to be slightly clearer about the matter. I must've used some other communication techniques to clarify the subject. But, I can't quite recall how I did it, it was very windy.

She smiled, nodded, displaying that the question was understood. She pointed to the bus stop, told me that it was the place where I had to wait. She'd understood the question alright, only I hadn't been able to express my concern. I needed to know more words than hello, thank you, & good-bye, to ask her whether or not the bus was gone already.

Either way, I thanked her, waved goodbye, slowly headed back to the stop. I was going through my options: I must catch the train from the town in a couple of hours, so I had to leave the village somehow in some ways. I realized there wasn't anything there to wait for, so I turned around before I finish processing the thought.

I hardly ever miss any of my rides: plane, train, or bus, maybe only a couple of incidents as far as I could remember. One of the trips was back when I was living in a remote village far down south. Technically, though, I didn't miss it. I was ready at the bus stop a few minutes earlier; my sunglasses were again on, the rucksack not so heavy on my shoulders. I waited. But, the bus didn't show up. I asked the locals who were starting their day by shooting coffee in the café on the other side of the square. They told me not to wait any longer; it was some kind of national holiday. Obviously, I was left clueless, without a single idea of how to leave that very small village. And of course, incredibly mad about the misinformation, that it hadn't been clear anywhere that the village buses wouldn't work on national holidays. Nobody even mentioned that it was going to be a national holiday in their country; how was I to know?! My time, then, was limited. I had to be quick; I had another bus to catch.

The bus was missed, & it was very windy. I could've been sitting on that bus if I hadn't wasted so much time earlier in the morning. If I hadn't snoozed for another five minutes after the alarm went off, if I had my coffee in the kitchen instead of taking it to the tulip. If I hadn't put my head in different trash bins along the way. A light headache struck me in the forehead because of constantly squinting and frowning to the sun and the wind regardless of my sunglasses; the wind was hurting me. Unlike the previous misfortune with the bus, I had enough time until my next ride. Besides, my bank account had shrunk visibly. Calling a taxi was off the table. I didn't actually have a local number to make the call, or enough skills on the language to speak to the driver. There was a payphone in front of the supermarket, but I didn't have a phone card either.

I might've mentioned before that I enjoy walking quite a lot. As a matter of fact, I was pleased that the occasion arose organically; such boiling morning would simmer gently. I walked on. Just very gradually, the cars parked by the houses, streets, alleys and people shifted into low hills, patches of trees in between farmlands, fields in different colors depending on what was planted; however, the sky would remain intact, and the shapeless clouds beyond the white storks and black crows. The gradual transformation of the view would clarify the rest of the day before my eyes without much effort. A new image was drawn now that the plans were inverted; for then, I would be walking.

As the last crumb of the village was put behind, which would be the cemetery with the dark-colored tombstones shining in the sun, I began to comprehend what a different notion it was to live so close to nature, to wake up by the sound of the birds living in the crowns of the trees. The most human noise was the occasional passage of the tractors going back and forth to the fields, & our interaction was a single rise of the hand as a warm distant greeting. Facing urban life after staying away for all this while was something to make me rather uneasy. It wasn't very long, I'd been living a reclusive village life for only over a season, though it was intense enough to make it feel like an eternity. The tranquility of the surroundings was so grand that traffic & honking horns, the siren of an ambulance disturbing my reveries, & people who would walk each other by without saying hello seemed to belong to another universe.

Yet, I would do nothing but to get used to it sooner than expected. I would rely on my good luck to befriend a local with whom I would be introduced to the Oldtown, take a walk, & appreciate a glass of wine in an ancient house; it could be a fitting cure for the loneliness. Nature, at least, leaves you no room to be lonely.

All of a sudden, I realized that the wind had stopped blowing, and was replaced by an occasional breeze; the frown upon my forehead had been washed away. It must've slowed down at some point, but I was too busy with the storm within that I really didn't notice. The sun was out, & it was now shining white through the clouds; it was making the air excellently warm. The sun was just the same as it was a few minutes before, but the heat wasn't sensible for the northern wind. After a few minutes of walking under the sunlight, I felt the rise of the temperature from inside. A bead of sweat got me to take off my jacket. I hung the jacket from the side of the bag, and readjusted the straps on my shoulders. Shook my head lightly, let the gentle breeze brush my hair back.

There were trees here and there on the side of the road which were casting a lovely shadow on the road. I walked across the road to stay under the shadow, the sun was getting a bit too warm. A couple of minutes of sunlight would've been enough to get heated through. I switched the lane to the shadow again, it was getting hot a bit too quickly. Sometimes the line of the shadow would be too long, & it would feel cold with the breeze. There's nothing worse than a cold shadow on a spring day, especially when you know the warm sun is right out the shade, you only cannot manage the temperature. I kept bending my way from one side to the other. It was hard to keep a balance, to keep the cold and the heat on a straight line. I started walking in the middle of the road to be exposed to both a little bit at a time.

The village was far behind. The sound of the cars echoed in the distance. Only a car or two had passed by. I walked by the lake passed the graveyard, wondered if there were more ponds beyond the view. There was an empty field in front of the lake with a very rich brown soil; it was almost red. It was covered with the thinnest layer of adoring baby leaves. They would soon fully grow, make it green all over, briefly topped with flowers in different colors, white, or bright yellow. Regardless, their warm smell would overflow the land, intense enough to fill up your nose just as you walk by; a full breath in would blow your mind. Too bad I wouldn't know the name of the plants, what the flowers were called. I could've collected a leaf to ask a professional later. Certainly, I would forget the name soon, but it would be nice to hear it at least once.

I could've taken a picture to look it up later—I still had a fairly dysfunctional smartphone in my pocket. A moment of spring could've been captured in a frame, but I really didn't bother. I found it a bit pointless; photographs don't smell, & the colors differ from reality, even the slightest bit. They wouldn't carry the same notion when you see the image elsewhere. Instead, I would simply watch the flowers, smell them in the air, & leave the moment uninterrupted. I let it be engraved in my memory, genuinely hoping it would come across my path once more. I look forward to experiencing the perfect timing of random incidents, live the raw flow. But then again, you never know which lane of actions you're in, so you might never know what you've been missing—it's not really a bus schedule written down on a piece of paper. The universe has a mysterious way of working things. It grabs you, churns you in such a numbing ride you can hardly tell how reality formed before your eyes.

I grabbed the shoulder straps of the rucksack, readjusted it on my back, & kept walking. The bag felt heavier since I'd left. It couldn't be just for the jacket, was it really that heavy?!

I didn't have an idea how far I'd gone. Seemed like a lot, but it surely wasn't. As I checked the map a few weeks after, I realized it was indeed quite a short walk. The path shrinks when you go through it for the second time. Shrinks even more on the third passage, or when you're on your way back. It doesn't make sense in reality; it's the same number of steps on the step-counter. Certainly, though, there's a magic to it; the path of going and returning is not the same.

It was the first time I was walking beyond the lake. The road felt new on foot, as if I was seeing it all for the first time, which rather added up to the length of the walk. The bag as well; it would've been a different experience if I'd packed lighter. Though, I promised to stay light for this trip. I honestly didn't take much, only a few items. It made me question what I put in it.

The weight of the bag was taking away my patience. I kept readjusting it on the shoulders, fastened the belt to make it more comfortable, although, in actuality, it didn't make much of a difference; the weight wasn't going anywhere. I wondered if there was anything in the bag that I could discard, anything to make it lighter. If there was any food to eat, even though I was not hungry at all, or any liquids that I could drink, but nothing came to my mind. I really didn't have much going on there. I distracted myself with the blue sky, and the fluffy clouds that were shifting shapes constantly.

I heard a car approaching from the distance. I paused and looked back. Raised my arm to let them know that I needed a lift; I needed help. They didn't stop. They waved hello, however. It was a husband and a wife. I waved back and smiled. I kept on walking as I watched the car getting smaller in front of me.

According to my watch, it had been almost an hour since I'd started walking. I could feel my legs, my knees, & my hips moving from side to side with every step. It wasn't really a good sign. They say you're not supposed to feel your body parts unless they're in pain. I had walked long before, so I wasn't out of practice. The journey wasn't unfamiliar either; I'd passed it by before, only, on the wheel instead of the foot; things were much slower now. I had a couple of tricks in my sleeves to get the distance to seem closer, & I get to pick new tricks in every long walk.

Once, I went on an adventurous walk by the ocean during my stay in the village far down south. I was traveling about, visiting the surrounding regions; I ended up in a marvelous town by the ocean unplanned. I heard about the lighthouse on the most western point of the continent which used to be known as the end of the world; someone told me that the sunset looked charming from there. I hit the road first thing in the morning. Found my way through the tall cliffs, the yellow beaches, small towns, and villages from the distance. I would've finished the walk if everything had gone according to plan; things never go according to plan.

At some point, I calculated, with the pace things were going, I would definitely miss the bus back, the last bus back to the village, which ironically enough, I did in the end. So, I switched directions, & bended my path to the main road to hitchhike at least a couple kilometers of the way. This would distract me from the route that I'd drawn for myself. But, it was still adventurous, & it was still very beautiful. I left the ocean briefly to join the road for a lift.

The road was empty, yet another isolated one. I had estimated at least twenty minutes to see the first car passing. But to my surprise, a car pulled over in only a minute. There were two men. Both local, construction workers, who were on their lunch break. They offered me to join, which was an excellent idea. I could already taste the red meat with some rice and a simple salad on the side, with a dressing as plain as olive oil and flaky sea salt. I could smell the house wine, could hear it pour into my glass from the jug. It was excellent indeed. I should've had lunch with them now that I was going to miss the bus. My limited time on the plan forced me to kindly decline. I thanked them for the invitation, & told them that I needed to be elsewhere. They said they didn't have much time either. Otherwise, they would've dropped me off to my destination. I thanked them again, told them that the point was to walk. The destination was only an excuse. I remember that the rucksack was with me during that trip. It was probably holding the same items, more or less. The gray towel, a couple of black shirts, and a sweater; I was not aware that I've forgotten the flip-flops under the bed of the hostel I stayed the night before; my leftover cheese was still in the fridge. It was the dinner I had with some wine.

The road was unusually empty which somewhat worried me. I wasn't quite sure if I could make it to the train station on foot. There were still loads of time left, but my tired feet were slowing me down. I could've rested under the shadow of one of those trees in between the farmlands. I would stay near the road in case a car would come by. I would take off my shoes, lean my back against the tree; only a cup of tea was missing to make it my living room. However, I couldn't risk losing any more of my time; I had to catch the train.

I knew a good trick for keeping the walk easier once you start to feel tired. I would mark the nearest sign as if it was going to be the final destination: the end of the brown field, then the giant power pole, the two trees, and later the small bridge over the river. The road would take a turn from then on, so I couldn't set another mark. I had to reach the turn to see the rest.

Fifteen Minutes

I slowly walked back to the entrance hall to take a seat on one of the beanbag sofas in the left corner. I wasn't in a hurry anymore; I could take my time. Except for the last fifteen minutes that I had to hurry madly to get to the train station, deep down in the essence of it, it was a very slow day. Every step was taking me a good few seconds; a very long distance from my heel to the tip of my toes. I had to improvise a way out. My brain was still processing how all the tickets could be sold, that the train was completely full, and no space was left. How small was this train?! It was terrible timing.

The truth was, which I learned a few weeks after, that I could've taken the train. If the ticket seller was nice enough, she would've told me that I could still get on the train. I might not be able to take a seat, but I could still catch a ride to the destination. I could've simply told the conductor, as I would stand close by the window, that I hadn't been able to purchase a ticket. And they would've sold me one easily. The price might've been a bit higher, yet, I could've left. That was the last train, missing it seriously was not good news. The next train wasn't until the next day. I was forced to stay. Without a single clue of what could possibly be done, I took a step forward. A tricky riddle to solve indeed.

The departure board was in the middle of the wall above the arched doorways. It was black, and the information was typed in matte light green. It was full of names of towns, numbers of the hours of the trips, & which platform the train would leave from. My train was the third one on the list. It would leave in exactly fifteen minutes. I was going to wave goodbye.

The sofas were all occupied. Some people were snoozing, some others were resting with their eyes open, & some were sliding the tip of their fingers on the screen of their phones. There were some benches by the bookshelves a few steps further away, but they didn't seem to be as nearly as comfortable as the beanbag sofa. To be honest with you, I'm not a big fan of those sofas. As a matter of fact, I quite dislike them. I don't think I would ever put such a thing in my living room, because I find them anything but comfortable. But, I was exhausted, & they seemed to be the only soft spot to rest my person all throughout the train station.

It had been a long stormy week with no breaks. The last couple of days were almost sleepless. I needed to rest, put my legs horizontally so that the blood would float for a change; my feet had swollen so badly that I think they were at least one size larger. Ideally thinking, I needed to lie flat on the ground, stretch my back, tuck my legs in, or raise them upwards to lean them against the wall; I fancied grass field and a tree on a warm sunny afternoon. I spotted a corner by the drugstore which seemed to be uninterrupted; I sat on the floor.

The stones were cold, not very pleasant as a matter of fact, but the exhaustion was so intense that I couldn't care. I leaned my head against the wall behind me; I didn't move. The funky red bag was sitting by me quietly, but for some curious reason, it fell on the floor all of a sudden. As if my stuff needed to stretch and relax as well.

At some point in the morning, I had taken the time to place my things neatly inside the bag, even though I was in a great rush not to miss the train. Keeping it sorted on the inside had somehow become a habit. I made sure that things were not squeezed too much, but they were also placed tightly enough so that they would protect one another. During the day, I would displace things based on the circumstances and what was needed: the blue bottle, the black rain cover, or my trusty scarf. And if the call was quick, such as a pen, or the notebook, or the case of the sunglasses, they would be tossed back in carelessly. After a certain while, everything would be everywhere. It would get chaotic inside; for some peculiar reason, the bag would feel heavier when the inside is messy.

I slowly turned my look down to the funky red spilled on the ground. Physically speaking, it shouldn't differ if the bag was sitting up or not, it would still be touching the floor one way or another. It was only my way of appreciating it for holding it all together. And the red bag had exhibited such high performance; it was not expected at all. It had kept my stuff safe, and had my back warm and set. Not quite sure if it could still keep me company just as well if it was winter. Things do get chunkier in winter, jumpers and jackets, thermal trousers, & woolen socks. Although, it would also depend on what's packed. It can always get lighter, I for sure know all about that; an extra jumper would be considered luxury.

The summer wasn't there yet, but the air wasn't as cold anymore. It was often rainy, however, the wind would still be brutal every now and again. I would zip up the black jacket in the evening, & hang it on the side of the funky red when the sun was out during the day.

I lifted the red bag back up to have it seated next to me. I tapped on it twice to make sure that it wasn't going to collapse. It felt light, strangely enough, lighter than the day before. As if it was missing something. What was it that I was leaving behind?!

The names and the numbers were constantly changing on the departure board. The trips on the bottom gradually arose to the top. My train left without me. I asked myself the concerning question: what was next?! The most obvious answer was that I had to catch the next train. But the morning was a long way ahead; it was only early in the afternoon. If I explored through my thoughts, I would most definitely come up with something; no need to worry. I had loads of time. And I wasn't in a hurry; nobody was expecting me, & I didn't have to be anywhere, if there was somewhere to go at all. I hugged my knees into my chest, my feet were lifted off the floor, & my thighs and shins were being squeezed into my stomach. The tension in my muscles was slowly being released. I moved gently from side to side. Took off my boots, laid my legs in front of me, & bent forward to hold the soles of my feet with the palm of my hands. I rested my head on my knees. I kept stretching my person on every possible angle. It felt good, the gaze of the other travelers didn't. I have to admit, the way I was camping in the corner of the train station by the pharmacy did feel rather lonely, the way some people noticed me and looked away to pretend they hadn't. I couldn't care much at that particular moment. I was tired, mentally, physically, or any other dimension there ever is to the human condition.

Generally speaking, it had been a while that seemed to be getting lonelier more than ever, sometimes a bit too often.

I had found tricks to surpass the feeling. An instant remedy was contacting a friend where I'm always welcomed in their company; the good news is that they're as far as my phone in my pocket as long as I have one. A picnic could make things look better. And I could set up one anytime, anywhere: sunny or not, in the morning or past midnight, on a meadow full of fresh yellow dandelions or on the rocks by the river. It felt home when I picnicked, I came in peace with however the mood was. Sad, or happy; sometimes it's okay to be lonely. The corner of the train station wasn't the most ideal place, but I guess that's the best I could improvise. That's really all you could do for yourself in life: make a corner of peace to live free of any judgments. You could then eat like a beast, wear whatever you fancy, party however you'd lose your mind the best, & adjust the bitterness of your coffee to your liking; everyone makes coffee differently.

Speaking of which, I was madly thirsty for coffee, or some black tea. But I wasn't really drinking anything, not even water. It wasn't another experiment to see how far I could go without drinking any liquids, I was avoiding drinking so that I could avoid visiting the toilets. You see, drinking equals the bathroom. And I was in a city. Public toilets might not be in the cleanest condition. I was also low on tissues in my pockets. I'd usually ask cafés and restaurants if I could use their restroom in case of an emergency; some café owners wouldn't let you use their place, which, quite frankly, is out of my mind; it's only a toilet. I'd try to find a fast-food restaurant chain; the toilet is almost always open to the public. Some big grocery stores are quite generous as well; not only with their toilet facilities, but also their network connection; it's unlimitedly free. Sometimes, however, you end up in a town where there are no cafés or restaurants, & the shops are too small to offer you a toilet.

On the flip side, such a thing can never be an issue in nature. In fact, it's quite nice to go in nature. You would have different options depending on your overall mood. You can have your personal space by a tree, next to a giant bush with yellow flowers, under the blue sky, or the twinkling stars if it's late at night. The bathroom would be blessed differently on every occasion. You only need to make sure that you have a shovel with you, just in case. And enough toilet papers. In nature, or in the city, you never know when you might need one. It's always a good idea to have some toilet papers in your pocket, for accidentally spilled drinks, or a runny nose, to wipe your hands after your picnic. I'd usually take the tissue I was given in the restaurant with my meal. I simply remove the corner that I cleaned my lips with, and keep the rest for later instead of dumping it onto my plate. I sometimes take an extra napkin as I wash and dry my hands in a restroom just to have the future secured.

I took the smallest sip of water out of my blue bottle, which was almost empty, to get passed the idea of tea and coffee. I took a deep breath, & released the air off my lungs slowly. It was hard not to think about it now that the idea was planted in my head. It's almost impossible to un-think, unless you're distracted by another thought. Once you know about it, you can never un-know it. You may forget about the information, but it is still there in the brain. Being aware of the fact would probably affect your thoughts and concerns in the future, therefore, you might exhibit different behaviors. Ignorance might be bliss; it might as well be an open gate to hell.

Take the toilet situation as an example. You'd visit a toilet, & would realize there are no toilet papers once you're done with your task. You'd be stuck, so you'd have to improvise another material to subsidize the missing item. Perhaps a plain piece of paper, or in absolute scarcity, even the receipts from the grocery store might do the job. Having the knowledge that you might be left without the toilet paper is perhaps essential to keep an extra tissue in your pocket as a precaution, but only a fair amount of the knowledge. My reality would differ from the scary stories that happened to the people visiting the bathrooms without toilet paper. It's a privilege not to know everything. It takes a lot to gain the skill of distinguishing the fine line which everything else beyond would be too much, in order to move based on the experience developed by the decisions made under the given circumstances. Otherwise, the flow would be broken. It then gets intimidating to make new moves, scary to try new paths once you're aware of all the possibilities that are about to come, which might not even happen in the end. You may do anything to avoid the situation; you may end up with tissues in every pocket you've got: trousers, jackets, jumpers, you name it. I'm not just talking about public bathrooms when they're out of toilet papers. Of course, it's essential to clean up after yourself, but no permanent damage is done if you're out of it.

The same logic applies to almost everything else. Sugar, for instance, I still can't get my head around it. Many shreds of evidence prove that refined sugar is bad for health. The perfect diet relies on natural sugar in fruits and vegetables to provide the body's daily dosage. No more, or your health would be in danger in a long run. But, what about the pleasure of a small pudding after dinner every so often?! What would a birthday be like without a chocolate cake?! It's proved that humans can go on without food for over forty days. Quite impressive to know how strong a human body is, to know that death doesn't come for over a month. Imagine the amount of time you'd be saving once you stop eating, the amount of money that won't be spent on grocery shopping anymore. However, life is a bore without eating. It's a very cold home when the kitchen is not running. The everyday routine would limp once you don't cook, once you don't do the dishes.

As I was rendering these thoughts, my stomach started to howl loudly, complaining how I could leave it empty for such a long time. Over twenty hours, I was counting the hours with my fingertips. The noises were so loud that I'd be terribly embarrassed if anyone was sitting next to me. I was hungry, but

I didn't feel like eating. I didn't care about food for some bland reason. I could correlate the appetite to the extreme exhaustion. My body probably had enough stored fuel to keep functioning; the only problem was my upset stomach that had been left empty for so many hours.

I'd lost interest in food for the last few weeks; things didn't really taste the way expected. I fancied barley soup with milk, followed my mother's recipe. That would've taken away my exhaustion in a blink of an eye. I tried to think of some food that I could've bought from a canteen nearby, or from the supermarket across the street, which would resemble the taste of the soup I fancied. But, nothing came to my mind. What could I possibly buy to take the place of the tender meat of the celebrated beef stroganoff, the savory béchamel sauce with mushrooms on top of the crispy shredded potatoes?! I'd been so far off that I didn't even care for potatoes anymore, fried, mashed, baked, whichever. Even if I had such a dish in front of me at that moment, I don't think I'd be able to eat it. It would taste dusty in that train station; I would never want to spoil the good memories of having it over a casual lunch gathering, the feeling of a warm hug I was given once I was done with the meal.

I wondered if it was time to head out, if I'd recharged enough to leave the train station for then. Ordinarily, I would look for a nice spot to picnic. And I've had quite a few picnics around the town to already have a usual spot or two. Though, it was not an ordinary day. I imagined that the benches by the river would be a nice place to hang about for a while, the pink ones under the bridge; it was a bit far away, but I would remain protected from the potential rain. It didn't seem like it would, but you'd never know when the rain might pour; the weather forecast couldn't really be trusted. It would still feel nice to be sheltered. The view was also very pleasant, the water running in front of you with the Oldtown standing beyond.

The only thing that was giving me a second thought was the wind, the occasional brutal wind of the spring. The weather wasn't picnic-friendly. It was cloudy, windy, & relatively cold. Not too bad to make the eating impossible; it just wouldn't be as enjoyable. I believe I had a picnic there not so long ago which was constantly interrupted by the wind. My solution was to simply zip my jacket up, put the hoodie on, cover my neck with my trusty scarf; the one item impossible to live without. It became rather tolerable, then. Not the best picnic ever, but I didn't let the weather stop me from enjoying the lunch.

The food was a pleasant surprise, now that I remember. I thought I'd bought something, turned out I'd purchased another thing. I couldn't read the label really. It was a supermarket food, two giant meatballs freshly packed in a plastic plate. Although, it was discounted by fifty percent; the freshness of the meal was highly questionable. Seemed like a reasonable deal, so I picked them up. I'd assumed that plain meatballs would be rather boring. So, I paired it with a small cucumber and some peanuts for the crunch. I picked an apple just in case I fancied some pudding after my meal. I used to keep an apple in my bag for many years; it would complement the component inside the best.

I'd sat on the benches and watched the river run in front of me. As I took the first bite off the cold meatball, I noticed that it was not only meat inside the ball, hidden was a hard-boiled egg. What a nice surprise indeed. Although, in my perfect world, the yolk would've been creamy, runny, and velvety with decent stress on the letter v.

I didn't eat the apple in the end, nor the peanuts; they remained untouched in my bag, saved for dinner, or tomorrow lunch. Having the river underneath my footsteps was sweet enough to be called the pudding. In another picnic, I'd replaced the dessert by taking a dip in the water. And another time, I took a nap under the sun on glossy soft grasses of an open field, where I'd kept my eyes shut to watch the pale orange light behind my eyelids fade into white, red, orange, and white again. But that's only a summer pudding, the privilege of heat; I must remain patient to get there. To be as carefree, cheerful as a dog that woke me up by licking my napping face in a park; another town, another picnic. It took me a few seconds to distinguish the dog's tongue on my skin, wake up, make sure it wasn't a dream. The owner apologized about it over and over. It was quite alright; it was time to get up anyway.

 I reached for my pocket to see how much money was left, and if there was enough for a cup of tea. I had drunk the blue bottle empty, I was still thirsty. Black tea cleanses the pallet, my grandparents would believe, it could completely wash away the thirst. I'm not so sure if the same thing applies to coffee as well. In certain cultures, coffee is served with a glass of water on the side. Whatever purpose the water serves, it's a nice touch.

 Black tea it was! My person would appreciate its warmth on a cold day like that. It got a bit confusing for a second there. In the desert, people drink hot tea in the hottest hours of the day to keep the body cool. In colder regions, tea is known as a warming beverage. It's a mystery how it could actually work both ways. It is lovely in winter, just as it is on a hot day. Black tea can be the magic potion everyone has been looking for. Though, it's really not.

 As I was counting the coins, & calculating the costs for the rest of the trip, the sound of a piano distracted my thoughts. I raised my head to look for the source. I saw a piano in the corner by the beanbag sofas. I didn't even realize there was a piano in the room; wouldn't it sound very ironic if I say my dream job was to be a detective?! An older woman was playing classical music; she was playing it wonderfully well. She had short white hair. Her back was slightly hunched over her skinny body. She seemed to be focused, obviously enjoying what she was doing. The sound echoed all over the hall, reached the high ceiling, & returned back down. I had seen pianos in train stations during previous trips; it was a genius idea. Once, it was a young man playing. I'd watched him from behind the glasses.

I started counting the coins again since I'd lost track. My skin was very dry, my hands weren't clean; my fingertips were almost black. I felt the dirt on my skin, I examined both sides. Hands could reveal a lot, if not more than the shoes. They'd let you know how hard times have been, they could talk about poverty, cold, or for how long they've been exposed to the sun. They could tell if life had been a smooth flow with soft peaks, or on the opposite side. My hands needed to be washed. I thought I might have some lotion somewhere inside the funky red, it just never occurred to me to use them in the past few days.

Once again, I sank into my corner. It was a mystery to me as well what exactly I was waiting for. For time to pass me by, perhaps to overtake me. Clocks were only shapes of the hands, or a combination of numbers. The sun was only the game of light and shadow, if it ever came out from behind the clouds. Nothing was going to happen, I wasn't expecting anything, so the wait didn't have much of a meaning to it. Yet, I remained put in my corner. I decided to wait for something. A short nap didn't seem like a bad idea. A micro nap, I'd better rephrase, where you'd keep your eyes shut for a few minutes to cross over to the other side without even noticing, only realizing that you've been away once you're awoken. However brief, it'd generate enough power for the house to keep up with the rest of the day. I hugged the eyes for a moment with my unclean hands; it sure was going to be a long day.

Then, I dedicate the wait for another song from the piano. Somebody would've come soon, would play a fine tune, and the stream of thought would shift. The piano was the best thing happening in the scenery; the hall was busy with humans, not too busy to make your head buzz, enough to have you confused where they were going. They were headed to the towns where the train was taking them to, the trips written in green letters on the wide black board.

The cold stones were starting to freeze my legs, soon it would spread all over. I should've grabbed the black jumper out of my bag, made it into my carpet now that the floor was bare. Too tired, I guess, that I couldn't be bothered.

The whole situation was a big misfortune, in a way, my bad timing had put me on another channel. If I'd arrived a few minutes earlier, I might've caught the last ticket on the train. Or if I'd asked another ticket officer, they would've informed me of the bonus information. I could've walked faster than that, even though I was almost running. Firstly, I could've left earlier if it wasn't such a slow morning. It took me long for some bleary reason. Some interesting event, or a funny story. At that point, I couldn't really tell what took me so long. The music ended, and the last note echoed all over the hall; somebody was playing the piano, they just left.

I stood up, gave my legs a quick shake to drop the dust off my cold legs. I paced aimlessly, the hall was small enough to leave the funky red alone. Took a walk to different corners to have a closer look at things. I stood by the bookshelves by the piano, full of books on different topics for different tastes, none of which I could read. I slowly walked to the piano as I stretched my arms and shoulders above my head. The piano looked old, but it wasn't antique to make its way into anyone's collection, it was just old. The body was in light brown wood with streaks of darker colors. I was intrigued to touch the keys. Very curious about the texture of the sound. But the instrument had an intimidating air to it that made me hold my distance.

There was a small shop in the corner, on the other side of the hall, where you could buy souvenirs and small tokens. The smell of coffee and sweets from the pastry led me across the hall. I noticed there wasn't much to eat. There was a set of stairs in the middle of the waiting room, in front of the tall glass doors of the platform, which would lead downstairs to other parts of the station. And there were people waiting all over.

I walked back to my corner in front of the pharmacy where the red bag was leaning against the wall. A cup of tea was missing off my hands. I would've wrapped my fingers around the cup to keep warm, would've sipped the hot beverage while thinking and pacing around the room. I remembered a couple of tea bags in my bag from a picnic very long while ago. I wondered if there was a way to get myself some hot water. How difficult would it be?! Logically thinking, it was only tap water heated to the temperature of one hundred degrees.

If I was able to speak the local language, I could've asked the lady at the pastry shop for this small favor. But, at that point, I was a tourist; life is different when you're a tourist. There was a grocery store not far away from the train station, which had a fully equipped coffee machine. It offered hot water as well. Hot tea was indeed an exciting idea. I picked the red bag off the floor, walked out of the train station on my happy feet.

I drew the route on my imaginary map. I remembered the park over the hill which was known for its perfect view of the sunset. Technically, it was on the way. I could fix my racy tea, return to the hill, & enjoy my drink watching the color of the sky change magnificently; seemed like a superb plan. The air felt nice. Even though it wasn't really warm outside, & the wind was harsh every now and then, I found it to be a very pleasant afternoon. Walking would've kept the body warm, & the mind clear. My legs weren't in their best condition.

I walked down the street, doing my best to take notes of my surroundings not to get lost. The streets and the alleys were still relatively confusing. I needed more time, more walking about to learn the paths and directions, more getting lost to know which way would lead where, & if there was any shortcut to it. I passed through the alleys, up and down, left and right. I noticed the monuments, churches, buildings, houses, shops, and spots that I'd been to before; the path was right.

I reached the avenue, realized that I still had a long way to go. My legs weren't walking with me, the soles of my feet were in pain. I was only a few steps away from giving up on the whole idea, and abandoning the perfect plan; I was about to crash where I was. I was tempted to settle for an ordinary coffee in a small bar I knew around the corner. I would, however, sit by the window on the tall stools to watch the street, the cars and the pedestrians, and the occasional trolley bus riding up the hill. I would order the usual: black coffee. Honoring an old habit practiced back in the south, I would ask for cinnamon to sprinkle on top of the crema to turn it a simple pudding.

I don't usually order tea in such cafés, tea bags are not really considered tea. There's no way to know what's inside the pouches, probably some paint and dust and artificial flavoring to turn the hot water into so-called tea. In order to make real tea, loose leaves must be steeped in a teapot on top of a kettle rolling on a gentle simmer. I'd taken the magic of black tea for granted, highly underestimated the power of freshly brewed tea. There was no joy, or any pleasure in ordering a tea bag in a café, especially now that I was alone; I could've gotten a cup of hot water and placed the teabag in it myself, which I was about to do, only, instead of The Greatest Place, I was going for a park with a nice view.

There was a bus stop just a few steps away in front of me. I wish I knew the town better to be able to take the bus. I really didn't know where I was headed to, the name of the district, or the street. However, all the buses seemed to be riding straight down the avenue till they reached the intersection where they switched paths; I could at least cast myself about fifteen minutes ahead.

I looked back. A big red bus was approaching the stop. I was fully aware that in order to make it to the bus, I should've picked up my pace, & started to walk faster. But, I didn't. I kept walking just as slowly. Even if the natural flow of things were uninterrupted, I would be presented with only two options: either, or. Catch the bus, or miss it. If I made it, it would've been an absolute win: I would've taken a ride, as I walked in my desired speed; I would've been on the right channel for a change. And missing the bus would be the result of the choice that I'd made: I had maintained the slow walk.

There were a few people waiting at the bus stop, I noticed as I got closer, whom I had to wait with; I missed the bus in the end. The digital information screen on the top left corner was announcing the next bus in fifteen minutes.

Seemed like a long wait, but thinking about it, it was only ten minutes, plus five more minutes; I still had sixteen hours to kill. The first few hours were going to be easy. In fact, I could've taken advantage of the time by getting some rest. Forget all the troubles, be me again. If the weather was for my benefit, I could stretch the picnic longer, enjoy the nap till the sunset to make it dark. Darker every minute, one level darker than the last episode. Things look different when it's dark. It gets colder, a striking reason to start looking for a shelter, somewhere safe. The streets are rather safe, unless the police start questioning you. For some shocking reason, it's illegal to stay on the street. I would be more concerned about the gaze of the people on their way to work in the morning. The park seemed to be a good idea. I only needed to make sure my clothes were warm enough, which I wasn't worried too much about either; there are always free clothes around the town, neatly folded in bags placed by the yellow clothing bin.

There are usually things to do in the early hours of the evening. People gather to catch up on each other's stream of thoughts, stories that took place while they were away. They gather to make new jokes for good laughs, to have a good time. Sometimes people may inspire each other by talking about how they perceive the surroundings.

People gather to feel less lonely. Life does get lonely from time to time. It goes on so as long as you're a human being. It storms you anywhere, in the busy city, or in the countryside. You may be walking, or having lunch, contributing to a conversation by mainly listening, dancing to zesty music at a party. It's only a state of being. Might be the brain's reaction to certain thoughts, past experiences blended in wrong assumptions and unrelated imaginations, lack of human interactions, or questions about mysterious games of reality. It could simply be a brew of irrelevant hormones making the wrong chemical reactions in the system. Truly a peculiar moment. Perhaps it's slightly less intense when you're in nature where you're treated rather differently; reasonably why it's less lonely. Nature makes you forget about you by drawing a bigger picture. Such small creatures we are comparing to the two-hundred-year-old tree, the grand waves of landscapes with the cities in between. We're only a spot in this frame.

It didn't take me long to get bored, bored out of myself, out of my mind. I stood up straight, moved my head from side to side as I scanned the street, twisted around the waist to check the bus stop, & see if anything was going on. There were trees around the road, bird fluttering amongst them. Cars were passing. People were walking, some were talking. It felt grim, but, in the end, it was a beautiful day. Things were happening, not very interesting to hold my attention for much longer. It was rather boring.

Luckily, I had the time on my watch. Time is the last thing to keep the mind busy before the boredom would kill you. The hands of the clock change place constantly. I could at least wonder what time it is. And simultaneously, get confused when I think about it twice, because there is no such thing as time; the universe doesn't have a watch on its wrist.

Time answers the most mysterious life events, things that wouldn't make sense in the present. Elusive moments usually fit the puzzle when taken a glance from the future. Time builds up the reality silently, reveals the secret of random. Its traces would

expose how it has passed: seasons, colors, the memorable dance in the living room as we sang happy birthday.
It was time to move on, I decided as I checked the time on my watch. Two minutes had passed already; it was indeed a very long while to spend on a moment that lacked a little something. It's an old saying amongst cooks and chefs, that it's always a pinch of salt when you taste something missing. Life in a broader sense, the way we understand and perceive it, has no pinch of salt. It felt to be one of those days where things were one step ahead, and I had to hurry. I didn't look back. The bus stop was left far away up the avenue.

I must've taken the wrong turn at some point that I ended up in an isolated alley; I was distracted, confused and mistaken by a building that I assumed I'd recognize. I followed the path to the end of the alley to realize that it would join another street, which was way off my route. It seemed rather familiar. I stood there for a moment, leaned against the wall, & took a good look around: I must've been there before. The wind was blowing gently, coldly, & irregularly. For a second, it went absolutely silent. One bird was singing. I zipped my jacket, squinted as I looked down the alley; it was empty. I could hear a car moving away in the back alley. The sound of the engine echoed until it reached me, but I didn't see anything. I was surprised how quiet it was for that hour of the day. Although, I couldn't tell for sure if it was late or early. The day was almost done for someone who's been up since four in the morning, still very early for the ones who just went to bed.

I noticed a hair on my sleeve, it was moving weightlessly with the wind. It didn't seem to be mine. I grabbed it with the tip of my fingers, & let it drift off in the air. I felt lost, but technically, I wasn't; there was no particular destination to arrive at, or any certain path to walk along. The initial plan was to pass the time, & make it the next morning. You don't really need a route for that, no maps needed, digital, printed, or hand-drawn. Nothing to fear once getting lost is off the list.

I reached a small bridge with a narrow river running underneath. I watched the water for a few seconds. I could imagine where it was going, joining the wider river of the town, but I really didn't know where it was coming from. Up the stream, there were hills covered in old trees. I couldn't see beyond, but it certainly looked beautiful. I was intrigued to climb up the hill, & see the other side. Not that day, no, not then. Perhaps you'd be interested to know that a few months after, we set a picnic with some friends a few kilometers up the river; it was beautiful.

At any rate, I couldn't overcome the curiosity of the view from up the hill. The lands were mostly flat, so even a small hill gives you a good look at the area. I wondered how long it would take me to be up there, fifteen minutes the most; it wasn't that massive of a hill. But, I was tired. You can't imagine how tired I was when I tell you I was tired. I wish I could put myself in a dream where gravity didn't exist, where I would float freely in the air. Glide, or swim in the room to get to the other corner. How easy life would be if we were constantly dreaming, living the way we fancy by just speaking our desires out loud to make them happen. Even if things went wrong, & somehow got out of control, we just need to take a deep breath, and remember to embrace it; nothing bad happens in a dream.

I crossed the bridge slowly as I kept my eyes on the water. It made me think of thoughts that vanished as soon as I tried to catch them. I needed to lie down to take some rest. I could set my bag on a branch of a tree, so the young leaves would keep it dry from the rain. Then, put me in the river, to let the water take me where it went. It's safe there in the water, I wouldn't be bothered by the strongest winds, or the cold storm, to worry about the fireplace in winter. There's a path drawn for the river. All there's left to do is to enjoy the scenery. I'd watch the sky, would imagine where the water would take me next, even though the future never looks as it's pictured.

It should all be about time, in the end. Time equals privileges. The time could be spent on a job, the work to pay you the income, to pay for your heating system. The same amount of time could be spent in the forest to collect woods for the fireplace. With your income, you could pay the bus, subway, or take a taxi; or you could spend the time walking. You could make a smart investment: buy yourself a bicycle; you'd cycle out the world. It's the same time, only spent differently. And time is limited. You have to watch out what it's being spent on, can't afford to waste it. The initial goal was to spend it most pleasingly. Sometimes, however, it doesn't happen; it's miserable. Sometimes you suffer. Perhaps you should, so that joy would make sense.

It might be a personal perception, but it passes by differently anywhere, depending on the land, & with whom it's being spent. It depends on the sun, what time of the year it is. If it's the summer where the sun doesn't really set, or whether it shines equally for every day of the year. Being an outsider, a foreigner, or a visitor might make the perception of time slightly more intense. The fact where you'd be gone soon, & most probably wouldn't ever return. Certain memories, then, make the time travel possible. Any object could remind you of the time gone by. You get to return with a thought, might bring a faint smile on your face. Time sweetens once it's passed.

The seconds of life were all left in the pocket to be spent.

A severe cramp in my stomach waved my thoughts away. It reminded me that I hadn't yet eaten. The stomach wouldn't sit back for a second. Logically thinking, the pain wasn't going away as long as I didn't treat myself with a proper lunch; breakfast, call it dinner for all I care. It was turning into a concern. Its absence was creating tension, limitation, some kind of stress because everyday life relies heavily on it. I believe I had an apple in my bag. Not that I would be worried about starving to death. It would be ridiculous to die out of hunger; the world is full of food. Too much of it in some places. If the country is drowning in poverty where food scarcity takes lives, then it's a different matter. Even then, humans are capable of learning how to live off of anything. The first step to adjust to the scarcity is to cut down on portions by picking smaller bowls, by using a smaller fork or a spoon. Even with all that, humans are generous with their food. Sharing is an act of love; what better way to show your affection by feeding a hungry.

Not the easiest thing when poverty becomes an everyday matter. However, once you face and accept the new poor reality, you'd be granted freedom on another dimension. It becomes somehow adventurous, if I dare to say so, you'd be introduced to the alternative plan. For instance, once, I gave a haircut to my friend Terhi and her son. In return, I was gifted a pair of handmade wool socks, & an incredible night. It was a winter's afternoon. November, as I recall, the fireplace was on, the living room was cozy, and it was totally dark.

Free food is almost everywhere when you look through the right angle. Whether it's collected from nature, or it's brought by the owner of the café of our very small town; salmon soup, meat pie, quiche, & cinnamon buns that we couldn't get enough of. Technically, it was illegal to give away the café's leftovers, they must be thrown away, but, who would throw away food?! Some of the most interesting foods that I had, now that I'm remembering things, came free. For most of the cases, other travelers and guests would leave their leftovers for the rest of the house when they parted: different cheeses, vegetables, sauces, or spices; everyone has a different shopping list. All of a sudden, we had random ingredients in the kitchen with which we would explore creativity infinitely.

I arrived at the park. It wasn't the part I had in mind, I must've entered from a different section. I imagined it was a higher spot on the same hill. The trees were old and tall. The top branches were making a very high ceiling. Just as if someone had closed the door to the room, the wind stopped blowing. I found a bench by a crooked tree, decided to settle there for a bit before I could get myself some tea.

A part of the town was seen from my seat, and a corner of the river. The sky wide open beyond, with the clouds and the sun soon to set. There was nothing to distract the view; I couldn't ask for more. I put the funky red down on the bench, made sure that it was near me. It was quiet. I took a deep breath in, inhaled the clean damp air. My inner face smiled, can't remember which thought elevated the cheer underneath my skin. I was taking a rest with my eyes open. It was getting darker. I could hear the inviting sound of the music far away in the distance; I would soon join the party. I leaned my back against the tree, & watched the sky in front of me. The sun was sinking, the colors were getting more and more intense.

Special thanks my family and friends for their support all the way through. Lovely people of Haihatus, Gullkistan, RAIZVANGUARDA, Freedom House, Buinho, Žeimai Manor House. I'd like to thank my dearest Hiten Utami for teaching me all about the good condition.

About the author

Sevda Khatamian, nineteen eighty-nine, her family was already living in Tehran when she was born in the month of July. Her father used to run his own business and her mother worked in a hospital. Later she became a lawyer. Soheil, her older brother, moved abroad right after he graduated from high school. Sevda took the same path and moved out of the country by the time she was eighteen.
After six years of living in Ankara, studying, working, and eventually living an unemployed life concentrated on personal creative projects, she decided to move to Istanbul, and discover life on another level, and back up new experiences.
She now travels as an artist in residence, and lives an experimental life in different countries.

Made in the USA
Middletown, DE
19 April 2022